The Romans in Scotland: The History and Legacy of Ancient Rome's Northernmost Campaigns

By Charles River Editors

A section of Hadrian's Wall

About Charles River Editors

Charles River Editors is a boutique digital publishing company, specializing in bringing history back to life with educational and engaging books on a wide range of topics. Keep up to date with our new and free offerings with this 5 second sign up on our weekly mailing list, and visit Our Kindle Author Page to see other recently published Kindle titles.

We make these books for you and always want to know our readers' opinions, so we encourage you to leave reviews and look forward to publishing new and exciting titles each week.

Introduction

Part of the ruins of Hadrian's Wall

"[The Romans] thinking that it might be some help to the allies [Britons], whom they were forced to abandon, constructed a strong stone wall from sea to sea, in a straight line between the towns that had been there built for fear of the enemy, where Severus also had formerly built a rampart." – Bede's description of Hadrian's Wall in the Middle Ages

The famous conqueror from the European continent came ashore with thousands of men, ready to set up a new kingdom in England. The Britons had resisted the amphibious invasion from the moment his forces landed, but he was able to push forward. In a large winter battle, the Britons' large army attacked the invaders but was eventually routed, and the conqueror was able to set up a new kingdom.

Over 1,100 years before William the Conqueror became the King of England after the Battle of Hastings, Julius Caesar came, saw, and conquered part of "Britannia," setting up a Roman province with a puppet king in 54 BCE. In the new province, the Romans eventually constructed a military outpost overlooking a bridge across the River Thames. The new outpost was named Londinium, and it covered just over two dozen acres.

For most of the past 1,000 years, London has been the most dominant city in the world, ruling over so much land that it was said the Sun never set on the British Empire. With the possible exception of Rome, no city has ever been more important or influential than London in human history. Thus, it was only fitting that it was the Romans who established London as a prominent city.

Londinium was initially little more than a small military outpost near the northern boundary of the Roman province of Britannia, but its access to the River Thames and the North Sea made it a valuable location for a port. During the middle of the 1st century CE, the Romans conducted another invasion of the British Isles, after which Londinium began to grow rapidly. As the Romans stationed legions there to defend against the Britons, Londinium became a thriving international port, allowing trade with Rome and other cities across the empire.

By the 2nd century CE, Londinium was a large Roman city, with tens of thousands of inhabitants using villas, palaces, a forum, temples, and baths. The Roman governor ruled from the city in a basilica that served as the seat of government. What was once a 30 acre outpost now spanned 300 acres and was home to nearly 15,000 people, including Roman soldiers, officials and foreign merchants. The Romans also built heavy defenses for the city, constructing several forts and the massive London Wall, parts of which are still scattered across the city today. Ancient Roman remains continue to dot London's landscape today, reminding everyone that almost a millennium before it became the home of royalty, London was already a center of power.

The Romans were master builders, and much of what they built has stood the test of time. Throughout their vast empire they have left grand structures, from the Forum and Pantheon in Rome to the theatres and hippodromes of North Africa and the triumphal gates in Anatolia and France. Wherever they went, the Romans built imposing structures to show their power and ability, and one of their most impressive constructions was built on the northernmost fringe of the empire. Shortly after Emperor Hadrian came to power in the early 2nd century CE, he decided to seal off Scotland from Roman Britain with an ambitious wall stretching from sea to sea. To accomplish this, the wall had to be built from the mouth of the River Tyne – where Newcastle stands today – 80 Roman miles (76 miles or 122 kilometers) west to Bowness-on-Solway. The sheer scale of the job still impresses people today, and Hadrian's Wall has the advantage of being systematically studied and partially restored.

Of course, the masterful architecture of the wall belied the fact that it was built for defense, because Scotland (known as Caledonia to the Romans) was never fully conquered or incorporated into the Roman Empire, a fact that many modern Scots remain quite proud of today. While the Romans made several efforts to subdue Scotland, it is not entirely clear whether their failure to complete the subjugation of the northern part of the British Isles was due to the ferocity of the Caledonian/Pictish tribesmen or whether the Romans simply came to the conclusion that the region had far too little to offer in the way of resources (either minerals, metals, or slaves) to warrant repeated major campaigns. Scotland in the 1st century CE had no settlements of any size, so profitable trade was not easy to establish, and so, did not offer any major motivation for military conquest. A further disincentive to any Roman general looking to achieve a decisive or speedy military victory was the terrain. Unlike much of England which, although forested, was relatively flat and so allowed for roads to be built, Scotland was both wooded and mountainous.

Scotland today, as then, is essentially divided into four distinct regions. What is now known as the Borders was during the time of the Romans densely wooded, and the Southern Uplands added to the obstacles faced by any military force moving into the area. The second area, the Lowlands, was crisscrossed by a number of major rivers, including the Clyde, the Forth and the Tay. These permanent geographical features made north-to-south travel especially problematic. The areas around the rivers were also marshy, making any building extra difficult and risky. The Highlands, as the region's name suggests, is mountainous, and travel was restricted to the few mountain passes through the glens. These glens were ideal places for ambushes, which is something the Romans learned the hard way. The fourth region is collectively known as the Islands and was made up of hundreds of small but inhabited islands in the Outer Hebrides, Inner Hebrides, the Orkneys and the Shetlands. None of these areas lent themselves to the normal Roman method of march, consolidate, and build roads that had proved so successful elsewhere.

The lack of settlement centers also made it difficult for the Romans to operate as they had done throughout much of the rest of Europe (including southern Britain). Their tactics normally involved occupying the major population centers, fortifying them, and then Romanizing them. Whatever the reasons, it remains that Scotland was never totally conquered. The major Roman occupation lasted no more than between 40 and 80 years, with the span being dependent on how 'Scotland' is defined. Alistair Moffat, a prominent Scottish historian, reached the firm conclusion: "The Romans left us nothing of any enduring cultural value. Their presence in Scotland was brief, intermittent, and not influential on the course of our history".[1]

Some of Moffat's conclusions might be justified since the Roman presence was intermittent and spread over a number of centuries. However, assumptions about the Romans abandoning Scotland after the failure of the Antonine Wall (known as the *Vallum Antonini*) to contain the natives is inaccurate. Construction began in 142 CE and stretched across what is now known as the Central Belt of Scotland, between the Firth of Forth and the Firth of Clyde. The Antonine Wall was a turf fortification, measuring approximately 39 miles, and was intended to mark the northernmost frontier of the Roman Empire. However, after several unsuccessful campaigns were launched to subdue the area, the Romans eventually came to regard the more famous Hadrian's Wall (begun in 122 CE) as the "true" northern border of their empire.

Even so, that does not mean that the Romans did not exert significant influence on the course of Scottish history, or that they did not impact on Scottish culture. *The Romans in Scotland: The*

[1] P. 226, *Before Scotland: The Story of Scotland Before History* by A. Moffat (2005). London. Thames & Hudson.

History and Legacy of Ancient Rome's Northernmost Campaigns examines the history of Rome's spread across the British Isles, and the manner in which they were stopped in Scotland. Along with pictures depicting important people, places, and events, you will learn about the Romans in Scotland like never before.

Scotland Before the Romans

At the time of Julius Caesar's first visit to Britain in 55 BCE, Romans knew very little of this mysterious land, and myths and legends about the fearsome Druids and blue-painted savages abounded in the Roman world. By the late 1st century CE, Britain was securely established within the Roman Empire and becoming an increasingly important and wealthy province that ultimately produced Roman Emperors of its own. The transition from a wild misty backwater into this wealthy addition to the Empire was not without difficulty. Rebellions, particularly those staged by the Iceni, were frequent occurrences. The savagery of these rebellions was such that it is difficult to understand how Roman rule was not only preserved, but how the process of Romanization, proven more successful in Britain than in most non-Latin provinces of the Empire, was achieved.

The reasons behind this success lie in the nature of the island's political situation, which facilitated a Roman policy of divide and rule. This was used in successful combination with their normal carrot and stick approach to pacifying what, for all intents and purposes, should have been an impossible challenge, seeing as how the Romans were operating so far from their center of power. The Britain invaded by Caesar in 55 BCE was populated by a large number of Iron Age tribes, all of which belonged to a broadly Celtic culture. In the context of Britain, however, the term "Celtic" must be seen as a linguistic one, because despite suggestions of deep-seated cultural links with the Celts of Northern Gaul, there is, in fact, very little evidence of permanent, strong ties between the Celts in Britain and those in Gaul.

The Brythonic language spoken in Britain at this time was similar to that spoken both in Ireland and Gaul, all of which are considered Celtic. Nevertheless, while ongoing links between the various centers of Celtic culture may not have been quite as widespread as earlier scholars had presumed, it is inevitable that people sharing a relatively common language would also share at least some cultural features. Fitzpatrick wrote: "It is clear then, that there is no intrinsic 'Celtic' European unity and that the idea of a Celtic Iron Age Europe has developed in an almost ad hoc fashion. When examined critically, the central idea of being 'Celtic' may also be seen to be weakly formulated."[2] Tacitus believed the Britons to be descendants of migrants from throughout Europe. He concluded the Caledonians were descendants of German settlers, while those in Wales, he argued, came from Iberia, and those in the south from Gaul: "Their physical characteristics are various and this is suggestive, overall however, it seems reasonable to believe that the Gauls occupied this island lying so near to them."[3]

Scholars have long debated the nature of these movements, but whether they were migrations, invasions, or simply a process of "diffusion" is largely unimportant. What matters is that tribes

---

[2] P. 242, 'Celtic Iron Age Europe: The theoretical basis' by A.P. Fitzpatrick in P. Graves-Brown *Cultural Identity and Archaeology: The Construction of European Communities* (1996). Routledge: London.
[3] Tacitus, *The Life of Cnæus Julius Agricola*, 11.

from various parts of the continent did settle in Britain, including the Belgae, who appeared on the island in the 2nd century BCE. Julius Caesar describes this migration in his *Commentaries on the Gallic War,* using the assumed unity of the Belgae and their descendants across the Channel in the war against Rome as the excuse for his invasion in 55 BCE.[4]

There were trading links between the groups in Britain. Archaeological evidence suggests that from the 8th century BCE onward, Celts in Britain traded with their counterparts across the Channel, bringing new ideas on, for example, the manufacture of swords. Trade was not restricted to near neighbours, and evidence confirms that Phoenician traders began visiting the island at about the same time, too, bringing various Mediterranean products with them. Similarly, it is evident that traders from Scandinavia brought their produce to Britain. All of these visitors seemed particularly interested in the country's mineral resources and salt. Goods were imported from the Hallstatt culture and these, in particular, influenced art in Britain. From the 2nd century BCE onward, Britons made use of trading routes developed by the Romans through Brittany and southwest France to access Italian produce and Hengistbury Head in Dorset became the center for the importation of Italian wine.[5]

Some estimates put the population of Britain in the Iron Age as high as four million by the end of the 1st century BCE, with the greatest density in the southeast. The average life expectancy was around 25-30 years old, although the rates were lower for women due to the many deaths in childbirth. Between 400 BCE and 100 BCE, evidence suggests the development of regional identities, and populations rose steadily, as "growth of population was one of the factors which led to the crystallising out of well-defined social hierarchies accompanied, especially in the south, by a degree of territoriality."[6]

Far from being the painted savages depicted by the Romans, the tribes engaged in extensive trade and commerce. While coinage from around Europe was used for trading purposes by Britons, they also developed and minted their own. Tribal kings put their names on these coins in the continental manner, and there are examples naming, for instance, Tasciovanus from Verulamium and Cunobelinos from Camulodunum. A number of buried hoards have been found throughout England, all confirming both the use of native coinage and the very disparate number of tribes based on specific regional areas.[7]

The Britain that Julius Caesar began taking an interest in from 58 BCE onward was, then, a relatively prosperous land with a large population and numerous, successful—if comparatively small—regionally-based tribes. Caesar's determination to conquer Gaul totally and completely

---

[4] Julius Caesar, *Commentaries on the Gallic Wars*

[5] *Greeks Romans and Barbarians: Spheres of Interaction* by B.W. Cunliffe (1988). London.

[6] P. 598, *Iron Age Communities in Britain: An account of England, Scotland and Wales from the Seventh Century BCE until the Roman Conquest, 4th Edition* by B. Cunliffe (2010). Routledge: London.

[7] Coins in Context: coinage and votive deposition in Iron Age South East Leicestershire' by I. Leins (2007). *The British Numismatic Journal* Vol. 77, pp. 2-45.

brought his initial attention to those tribes in Britain, based on his assumption they were helping the Gauls in the war against Rome. His underlying focus, however, was always his long-term plan to take total control of Rome. To do that, he had to retain control of his army. To retain that control, he had to have an enemy the Senate perceived to be a real threat to Rome. Therein lies the basis of Caesar's attempts to paint the British, and especially the Druids, as barbarians able to threaten Roman civilisation. The tactics of demonization were not particularly new to the Romans—they had employed the same tactics in the wars against the Carthaginians (who were also accused of being practitioners of human sacrifice). For Caesar, Britain was never an end in itself, but simply a means to with which to attain his greatest objectives, which accounts for his relative lack of success in his invasions compared to his other military exploits. Nevertheless, he brought Britain into the Roman consciousness, and it was inevitable that at some point Rome would turn its full attention to the island.

Scotland was known to ancient writers as Caledonia, and the area was mentioned for the first time during the Greco-Roman period by Aristotle in *On the Cosmos*. He referred to two islands, Albion and Ierne (Great Britain and Ireland).[8] The Greek explorer and geographer Pytheas of Massalia (modern-day Marseille) is recorded by Strabo as visiting Britain sometime between 322 and 285 BCE.[9] After circumnavigating the island, he concluded, accurately, that it was triangular in shape. He also identified the most northerly point as Orcas, or Orkney. Originals of his book *On the Ocean* have not survived but are known to have existed in the 1st century BCE, as well as being recorded by later writers such as Diodorus Sicculus (91–30 BCE),[10] Strabo (63 BCE – 23 CE)[11] and Pliny the Elder (23/24–79 CE).[12]

From them, historians know that a basic knowledge of the geography of north Britain was available to the Romans from then on. The Roman geographer Pomponius Mela (15 CE – c. 45 CE) records 30 Orkney islands and seven Haemodae (now known as the Shetland Islands) in his work *De Chorographia* (written in 43 CE). His figures are well short but not outrageous, since there are 70 islands in the Orkneys and 300 that make up the Shetlands, so it could well be based on an actual visit or information provided by others who had. Roman pottery dating to before 60 CE has been found at the Broch of Gurness in the Orkneys, but it is impossible to determine if that is proof of direct contact between the islands and Rome or whether it arrived there in some other way.

The first controversy relating to Scotland at this time is who exactly lived there and from where they originated. The *Collins Encyclopaedia of Scotland* states that "the Picts did not 'arrive' – in a sense they had always been there, for they were the descendants of the first people to inhabit what eventually became Scotland".[13] Stuart McHardy supports this claim in his

---

[8] Aristotle, *On the Cosmos*, 393b12.
[9] Strabo, *Geographica*, II.4.1
[10] Diodorus Sicculus, *Bibliotheca Historica,* V.19-40.
[11] Ibid, I.4; II.3; III.2; IV.2, 4, 5; VII.3.
[12] Pliny, *Natural History*, XXXVII.

historical overview, arguing that "the Picts were in fact the indigenous population of this part of the world" by the time the first Romans arrived in Britain.[14] His contention is that they originated in Scandinavia and migrated first to the Orkneys, and then from there moved southwards into the north of Scotland.

Archaeological evidence about the Picts is scarce, but what there is does seem to confirm them as the indigenous people of this region. G. Noble concurs with his colleagues' view: "[a]ll evidence points to the Picts being indigenous to northern Scotland".[15] He goes on to say that "they began to coalesce during the late Roman period and formed some of the most powerful kingdoms in northern Britain in the early medieval period".[16] Whether the Caledonians who lived in the Lowlands of Scotland were one of a number of Pictish tribes or were a different ethnic group entirely is still not clear.

There is little controversy about how the population all lived. They formed relatively small communities and built homes out of wood. They also worked stone, as is evident from the engraved standing stones still extant, many of which can now to be found in Scottish museums.[17] These stones, if Pictish, would be the only record the Picts left of their history. All other contemporary information about them comes from Roman writers, and given the little extant physical evidence and other information deriving from arguably biased sources, modern historians have found it extremely difficult to piece together any coherent history of the Picts before Roman times. However, McHardy has no doubt that it must have been the Picts who built the megalithic structures scattered around the north of Scotland.[18]

The small communities in which the Picts lived were usually made up of families belonging to a single clan. Each clan had its own chief, and it is possible to identify some of these from Roman sources, including the Caerini, Cornavii, Lugi, Smertae, Decantae, Carnonacae, Caledonii, Selgovae and Votadini.[19] As essentially family units, known as *kin* from the Gaelic word for a child, they were inwardly focused and loyal to their own members but not above raiding near neighbours for cattle or whatever else they could steal. It was only when faced with a serious external threat, such as the Romans, that they came together in confederacies under a chief elected for the time of the specific emergency: "The head of the kin was a very powerful man. He was looked upon as father of everyone in the kin, even though he might only be a distant cousin to most. He commanded their loyalty: he had proprietary rights over their land, their cattle; their possessions were in a sense his. His quarrels involved them and they had to take part in them, even to the point of laying down their lives".[20]

---

13 'Picts'. In: *The Collins Encyclopaedia of Scotland* (eds). J.Keay & J. Keay (1994). London: Harper Collins.
14 C1, *A New History of the* Picts by S. McHardy (2010). Chippenham: CPI Antony Rowe.
15 Noble, G., 'The Puzzling Ancient Picts of Scotland', *Ancient History Et Cetera*. Interview by J. Wiener (29 November, 2013). [ONLINE] Available at: https://etc.ancient.eu/interviews/the-puzzling-ancient-picts-of-scotland/
16 Ibid.
17 Examples of such can be found in the National Museum of Scotland in Edinburgh.
18 P.33 *A New History of the* Picts by S. McHardy (2010). Chippenham: CPI Antony Rowe.
19 Ibid, p. 31.

The technology of everyday life was similar to that found in Ireland during the same period, and evidence has been found of watermills. Kilns were used for drying kernels of wheat or barley, and *brochs*, roundhouses, and *crannogs* dating from before the Picts continued to be used. Some wheelhouses may have been constructed for ritualistic purposes, especially in the west and north. Their locations are quite specific, indicating that they may have been part of a particular tribe's political or cultural needs and built by those using them rather than being pre-Pictish buildings taken over for that purpose.

The origin of the name Pict is problematic of itself. It has been suggested that it came from the fact that these particular tribesmen painted pictures or tattoos on their bodies. Another suggestion is that it is a Celtic tribal name and that the Scottish Picts may have been related to the Pictones of Gaul mentioned by Julius Caesar in his *Gallic Wars*.[21] The strong emphasis on kinship and the centrality of family has also raised the possibility that the origin of the name was from the word *pecht*, which meant 'ancestors'. McHardy cites the word *pecht* as "a general catch-all term for ancestors", and he references the historian W. Nicolaisen, who pointed out the similarity of the Old Norse word *pettir* and the Old English word *pehtas*.[22] Based on this, McHardy concluded it was unlikely that the Romans coined the term Picts.

For most of the period of their involvement in Scotland, the Romans referred to all of the tribes living there as Caledonii. The origin of the name is simple enough to understand, meaning the people "living in the land of Caledonia". Stefan Zimmer, a German linguist, argues that Caledonia comes from the name "Caledones", which he believes meant "possessing hard feet" and was a reference to the perseverance of the tribe.[23] He saw the root as being proto Celtic, adding weight to the argument that the Caledonians were distinct from the Picts. It was only from the late 3rd century CE onwards that the Romans began to identify the Caledonii as just one tribe of a larger people they began to call the Picts.

The term Picti, as meaning "painted", was first used in writing by Eumenius in 297 CE, though the basis for his claim is unknown.[24] Another theory is that "Pict" meant "unromanized Britons". However, these two explanations for the term's origin based on associations with the Celtic language are weakened by the fact many scholars have concluded that the Pictish language was not Celtic at all, whereas that of the Caledonians was. Historians of Scottish history have long debated whether the Caledonians and the Picts were of ethnically the same stock but under different names. However, the linguistic evidence does not allow for any such definitive conclusion since it is known that the Caledonians definitely spoke a Brythonic language, whereas the Picts may, or may not, have spoken a Brittonic language of some kind.

---

[20] P. 30, *The History of* Scotland by P. Somerset Fry & S. Somerset Fry (1982). London: Routledge.
[21] Julius Caesar, *Gallic* Wars, VII.4,6.
[22] P. 36, *A New History of the* Picts by S. McHardy (2010). Chippenham: CPI Antony Rowe. See also; p.150, *Scottish Place-Names* by W.F.H. Nicolaisen (1976). Batsford. London.
[23] P.163, "Some Names and Epithets in Culhwch ac Olwen" by S. Zimmer (2004). *Studi Celtici 3*. pp. 163-179.
[24] Eumenius, *Pro restaurandis*.

From what evidence there is, the two languages were very different. P. Salway believes the Caledonians were Pictish tribes that spoke a Brittonic language because of their proximity to northern British tribes.[25] It has also been speculated that Emperor Septimius Severus' attacks on Caledonia at the beginning of the 3rd century CE annihilated the Brythonic speaking tribes in the region south of the Firth of Forth. And if that is the case, then Moffat's claim that the Romans did not influence Scottish history is wide of the mark.[26] Supporting this notion further of the Caledonians being wiped out are the accounts for the ease with which Irish tribesmen were able to overrun Lowland Scotland. Whether the two were ethnically the same or not, the Caledonians certainly made up a separate confederacy of tribes living in southern Scotland during the Iron Age that may have been Celtic in origin. The tribes that could be said to be Picts were scattered across the whole of Northern Scotland, as far north as Orkney and as far south as the Firth of Forth. While they, too, may have been ethnically Celtic, it seems more likely that they were actually of Scandinavian descent.

It is difficult to describe what the average Caledonian or Pict looked like, but Tacitus (56–120 CE) in his biography of Agricola wrote that they were red-haired and large limbed, facts that he believed pointed to a Germanic origin.[27] Eumenius, writing 200 years after Tacitus, also noted that both Caledonians and Picts were red-haired.[28] Claudius Ptolemy, writing around 150 CE, identified a number of distinct tribes, including the Cornovii in Caithness; the Caereni, Smertae, Carnonacae, Decantae, Lugi and Creones, who all lived north of the Great Glen; the Taexali in the north-east; the Epidii in Argyll; the Venicones in Fife; with the remaining Caledonians located in the central Highlands; and the Vacomagi centerd near Strathmore.[29]

By Ptolemy's time, southern Scotland was occupied by the Damnonii in the Clyde Valley; by the Novantae in Galloway; by the Selgovae on the south coast; and the Votadini to the east. However, Ptolemy's identifications cannot be verified, and in the case of the Novantae, he is the only source that makes any mention of them at all. The plethora of tribes and confusion over the various languages they spoke, the controversies over whether they were Celtic or Pict, and whether all of them were ethnically the same, has made it difficult to pin down exactly who lived where and when. However, in general terms, the Caledonians and Picts comprised the major population units, and it is on them that most research has focused.

The Caledonians and Picts had much in common in terms of their tribal organization and general way of life. Hundreds of Iron Age sites have been discovered in Scotland dating to pre-Roman times. These remains indicate the population lived in stone buildings, now known as Atlantic roundhouses. There are at least 100 of these sites, and some still with extant foundations of towers and outbuildings as well. They appear to have been built over a millennium, from 800

---

[25] *Roman Britain* by P. Salway (1986). Oxford: Oxford University Press.

[26] *Before Scotland: The Story of Scotland Before History* by A. Moffat (2005). London. Thames & Hudson.

[27] Tacitus, *Agricola*, XI.

[28] Eumenius, *Pro restaurandis.*

[29] Ptolemy, *Cosmographia*, 1467.

BCE to 300 CE, with the largest, known as *broch* towers, dating from the 2nd century BCE.

There are few extant remains, but some examples provide sufficient material to conclude the walls were as high as 20 feet. The largest of these 100 are found on the islands of Barra and North Uist and would have been able to accommodate the entire population. No evidence has been found to link these buildings specifically with any elite social group or activity; indeed, there is little evidence of anything resembling an aristocratic class at this time. Similarly, there is no evidence of a priestly class, so it must be assumed that these structures were for the use of the entire community.

Some *broch* towers in southern Scotland date from the period immediately prior to, and after, Agricola's invasion, around 83 CE. 15 have been found in the Forth valley, close to the Firth of Tay, in the far southwest, and along the eastern Borders. Their existence so far from the main centers of *broch*-building is another mystery. The Leckie Broch was destroyed by the Romans, but there, and also on the site of Fairy Knowe at Buchlyvie, numerous artifacts both Roman and native have been found. They were both built in the late 1st century and were substantial buildings. Remains of sheep, cattle, pigs, wild game, red deer and wild boar have been found at both, signifying the high status and wealth of the occupants. Another feature of this period are the *souterrains*, over 400 of which have been discovered so far, mainly dating to the 2nd and 3rd centuries CE. Their use is not known but as they have all been found in the vicinity of settlements it is possible that they were some sort of food storage facility.

Dating the various forts found throughout Scotland with any accuracy has also proved to be difficult for archaeologists. Some of the extant forts that have been uncovered are vitrified (vitrified forts are stone enclosures whose walls have been subjected to vitrification[30] through heat). They are not unique to Scotland but are more common there than in any other part of Europe. Most of the forts were located on hills to command a strong defensive position. Their shapes were determined by the contour of the enclosed summits. Exterior walls varied in size, with some measuring over 12 feet wide; these are so broad that at first sight they seem to be embankments. Where considered necessary, sections of the defenses were able to be strengthened by the erection of double or triple walls, and in some instances ramparts, composed of large blocks of stones, encompassed the vitrified center. These structures were all built without lime or cement and constructed rather like dry stone walls where at some point heat was applied in order to fuse them together. There are examples where stones have partially been melted and calcined[31] but the edges of others are fused so that they are cemented together. It is very rare, however, to find the entire length of a wall to be vitrified. As with so many issues related to the activities at this time, it is not entirely clear why the tribes vitrified the walls. The process actually weakens the strength of the structures. However, it is highly unlikely that such a method would have occurred 'by accident', and current thinking is that vitrification was a

---

[30] This process specifically refers to the process of something changing into glass (or a glass-like substance).
[31] The process of calcination derives its name from the Latin word *calcinare* ('to burn lime').

deliberate act, possibly as a ritual closure of a site no longer needed. The absence of Roman artafacts suggests that the majority were abandoned well before Agricola's expedition.

Scotland in the Neolithic and Bronze Ages produced numerous funeral monuments, whereas Iron Age burial sites are extremely rare. As such, a normal source of evidence as to a particular culture is missing. The evidence for the extent of Roman impact on tribal culture is, in consequence, even more difficult to assess. The Votadini, who occupied the south-east of Scotland, are seen as the tribe most quick to accept Roman rule, but even in that area lasting evidence of Romanization is almost nonexistent. The hill forts that stretched from northern Britain into the Highlands constructed by the major tribes are different from their southern counterparts in a number of ways; they were much smaller than those found in the south (often being less than two and a half acres) and there is no evidence that they were permanently garrisoned.

For whatever reason, by the time the Romans arrived on the scene, there had been a definite move towards fortified farmsteads rather than hill forts as the main defensive structure, being somewhat larger and home to intermarried kinship groups. These farmsteads were not as easily defended as the forts but were relatively more pleasant places to eke out a living. One theory for this significant change is that there was less competition for scarce resources because the population was in decline or because food was easier to come by due to advances in agricultural techniques.[32] However, after Agricola's retreat there appears to have been a renewed wave of *broch*-building.[33] The absence of Roman artifacts at this site suggests that they were built by northern tribesmen filling the vacuum left by the Romans. It is also plausible that the native southern tribes built them themselves.

The Agricola campaigns resulted in a more comprehensive identification of Caledonian settlements, and Ptolemy's *Geography* identifies 19 of what he termed towns. However, no archaeological evidence has been uncovered of any settlement that might be classed as an urban center, and it may well be that the 'towns' named were actually hill forts or marketplaces. The location of these towns/forts is also unclear. What Ptolemy calls Devana may be the modern Banchory. Alauna, meaning 'the rock', could be Dumbarton Rock. Another place with the same name may be the site of Edinburgh Castle, while Lindon has been tentatively identified as Balloch on Loch Lomond.[34]

Every man, Pict or Caledonian, was expected to be a warrior, but all were also farmers and fishermen. Women were expected to work on the land as well as raise the children. Apart from the intermittent cattle raids mounted against other local tribes, on the whole, the evidence

---

³² Pp. 151-162, *'Understanding hillforts: have we progressed?' by Cunliffe, Barry (2006). In: Payne, A., Corney, M., & Cunliffe, B. (eds.), The Wessex Hillforts Project: Extensive Survey of Hillfort Interiors in Central Southern England.* Historic England in association with Liverpool University Press.
³³ Edin's Hall Broch in Berwickshire is the best preserved of these newer southern *brochs*.
³⁴ Ptolemy, *Geography,* II.2.

suggests that the Picts and Caledonians lived a relatively peaceful agricultural life, with the Caledonians appearing to have had more to fear from external enemies than the Picts. This is evidenced by the larger number of hill forts discovered in their region. Given Scotland's poor soil and lack of natural resources, life expectancy was short, and everyday existence extremely hard. After the first reference to the Picts in 297 CE, the tribesmen are mentioned in a number of written records up until approximately 900 CE. After this date, they merely merge with the Scots migrating from Ireland. As they had a written history by that time, the two histories simply joined together.

The Romanization of Britain

Andreas Wahra's picture of an ancient bust of Caesar

Caesar's expeditions to Britain in both 55 BCE and 54 BCE have to be viewed against the backdrop of the political situation in Rome at that time. Caesar had control of a large army in Gaul, and his campaign was, to a very large extent, undertaken on the pretext of combating an external threat to the empire. This justified the maintenance of his control over these forces at a time when there was a move in Rome for him to be relieved of his command even before the end of his commission, which was scheduled for 54 BCE.

Thus, Caesar was determined to retain command of his troops at all costs, which was pivotal to his political plans. As outlined in his *Gallic Wars*, he claimed the Britons had been aiding the Gauls and posing a very real threat to the Roman attempt to pacify the newly-conquered country.[35] The English Channel was generally regarded by the Romans as defining the very edge of the world, and the symbolic significance of crossing the "Ocean" was not lost on Caesar, intent as he was on projecting himself as Rome's greatest general and politician.

The first invasion began in the late summer of 55 BCE, despite the fact that it was already very late in the campaigning season. Gaius Volusenis was sent in a single ship to scout the south coast area as Gaulish merchants had refused to provide any information about Britain to the Romans. He did not land, as "he did not dare leave his ship and entrust himself to the barbarians."[36] The scouting expedition lasted five days and furnished with what little information his tribune had been able to gather, Caesar planned his invasion. Various tribes in the south of Britain grew alarmed as soon as they realized the Romans were intent on invading, and a number of tribes sent envoys to Caesar, offering their submission. He sent these back to the island along with his ally, King Commius of the Atrebates, to win as many tribes over as possible before he landed.

The invasion fleet numbered 80 transport vessels with the capacity to transport the Legio VII, the Legio X, and other fighting ships, and the fleet was assembled at what is now Boulogne, then known as Portus Itius. In addition, Caesar arranged for a further 18 transport ships to take the cavalry from Ambleteuse after he had landed.[37] The fact that Caesar was in something of a hurry is exemplified by the fact he set sail well after midnight on August 23, 55 BCE, without the cavalry, any siege weapons, or any of the baggage assumed necessary for a serious attempt at conquest.[38] This lack of detailed planning has led many historians to conclude that Caesar did not intend the expedition to be one of total subjugation.

Whatever the original aim, it is clear the Romans had initially intended to land at Dover, but upon arrival offshore, the numbers of assembled tribesmen on the cliffs persuaded Caesar that discretion was the better part of valour, and he sailed a further seven miles up the coast to what

---

[35] Julius Caesar, *Commentaries on the Gallic Wars*, 4.20. (Trans. by W. A. McDevitte and W. S. Bohn) [Online]. Available at: http://www.forumromanum.org/literature/caesar/gallic_e1.html

[36] Julius Caesar, *Commentaries on the Gallic Wars*, 4.22. (Trans. by W. A. McDevitte and W. S. Bohn) [Online]. Available at: http://www.forumromanum.org/literature/caesar/gallic_e1.html

[37] P. 19, *Britannia: History of Roman Britain* by S. Frere (1987). Routledge: London.

[38] Julius Caesar, *Commentaries on the Gallic Wars*, 4.30. (Trans. by W. A. McDevitte and W. S. Bohn) [Online]. Available at: http://www.forumromanum.org/literature/caesar/gallic_e1.html

he thought was an unguarded beach—now thought to be Pegwell Bay on the Island of Thanet—and landed there.[39] The establishment of a beachhead proved extremely difficult, as the British fiercely opposed the landings and were only driven back by ballistae fired from ships anchored off the coast.

A camp was established. Caesar received hostages from the surrounding tribes, but he was unable to consolidate his bridgehead as his cavalry did not arrive. He quickly realized he had not come equipped to deal with a typical (harsh) British winter. Aware of his precarious position, Caesar decided to return to Gaul rather than risk being stranded in Britain over the winter with the very real possibility of complete defeat. He successfully crossed back to Gaul and continued to receive hostages from two tribes on the southeast of the island. The other tribes, however, believed the threat from Rome to be over and decided not to honor their pledges.

No matter how this particular campaign is assessed—either as an intended invasion or a reconnaissance mission—it failed to achieve any real goals. Despite this, the Senate, awed by the fact that Caesar had gone beyond what they regarded as the "known world", declared a supplication—or thanksgiving—of 20 days in honor of his achievements.

On his return to Gaul, Caesar immediately began to plan for a second invasion, scheduled for 54 BCE. Cicero referred to these plans in letters to a friend, asking him to make sure he acquired a British war chariot for him.[40] The Romans had learned from their mistakes in 55 BCE, and instead of invading with only two Legions, on this occasion, the force was comprised of five plus 2,000 cavalry, and all personnel were carried on ships specially designed for beach landings. He also planned his supply route more carefully and leaving Labienus at Portus Itius to oversee the regular transport of all food and other equipment necessary to maintain an invading force.

The Romans landed at the spot Caesar had identified the previous year, but this time their landing was unopposed. As soon as the bridgehead was established, Caesar ordered Quintus Atrius to advance inland. By the end of the day, this force had covered nearly 12 miles and defeated a British force at Bigbury Wood.[41] The next day, the Romans prepared to march further inland, but a severe storm that wrecked numerous invasion fleet vessels caused Caesar to order his troops back to the coast for repairs.

In early September, Caesar marched inland once again, confronting the forces of Cassivellaunus, the king of a tribe living north of the Thames. Cassivellaunus had recently successfully defeated the Trinovantes and was now their war leader, as well. With a combined force, the Britons harried the Romans but realized they were not strong enough to inflict a decisive defeat on the invaders. Caesar continued his progress northwards, but the constant

---

[39] Julius Caesar, *Commentaries on the Gallic Wars*, 4.25. (Trans. by W. A. McDevitte and W. S. Bohn) [Online]. Available at: http://www.forumromanum.org/literature/caesar/gallic_e1.html
[40] Cicero, *Letters to Friends*, 7.6 and 7.7.
[41] P. 22, *Britannia: History of Roman Britain* by S. Frere (1987). Routledge: London.

attacks meant that by the time he had reached the Thames, that one, fordable crossing had been heavily fortified by the Romans who had used an elephant to terrify the Britons and the defenders into abandoning the crossing due to fright.[42] The Trinovantes sent ambassadors promising aid and provisions against Cassivellaunus and the Romans restored Mandubraccius to the Trinovantine throne. Other tribes followed the Trinovantine lead—including the Cenimagni, the Segontiaci, the Ancalites, the Bibroci, and the Cassi—and surrendered. Caesar, now in a more secure position, laid siege to Cassivellaunus' last stronghold at Wheathampstead.[43]

As in the previous year, Caesar was eager for a resolution to the conflict and was fearful that he would be stranded in Britain over the winter. Consequently, he did not press the siege, and when Cassivellaunus offered to provide tribute and hostages and agree not to attack the Romans' new allies, the Romans agreed to the terms and promptly left the island. No garrison of any sort was left in Britain to enforce the settlement, and it is not known if any tribute was ever paid.[44]

While both of Caesar's two invasions failed to produce military or economic advantages, the second foray provided the Romans with a significant amount of knowledge about the island that they did not have prior to the campaigns. Geographical knowledge was collected, not by Roman advances, but in dealings with local populations. Caesar's discoveries were limited to Kent and the Thames Valley. In his *Commentaries on the Gallic War,* however, Caesar made note that "[t]he climate is more temperate than in Gaul the colds being less severe." He also wrote, "The island is triangular in form and one of its sides is opposite to Gaul. One angle of this side, which is in Kent, whither almost all ships from Gaul are directed, looks to the east. The lower looks to the south. This side extends about 500 miles. Another side lies toward Spain and the west, on which part is Ireland is less, as is reckoned, than Britain, by one half, but the passage from it into Britain is of equal distance with that from Gaul. In the middle of this voyage is an island which is called Mona many smaller islands besides are supposed to lie there, of which islands some have written that at the time of the winter solstice it might be night for thirty consecutive days. We, in our inquiries about the matter ascertained nothing except that, by accurate measurements with water, we perceived the nights to be shorter there than on the continent. The length of this side, as this account states, is 700 miles. The third side is toward north to which portion of the island no land is opposite but an angle of that side looks principally toward Germany. This side is considered to be 800 miles in length. Thus the whole island is about 2,000 miles in circumference."[45]

The actual total circumference of the island, taking account of inlets and so on, is actually about 11,000 miles, but Caesar's figures denoting the approximate shape of the island are extraordinarily accurate. The ability to assess potential landing sites and harbors proved

---

[42] Polyaenus, *Strategems*, 8.23.5.
[43] P. 25, *Britannia: History of Roman Britain* by S. Frere (1987). Routledge: London.
[44] Caesar, *Letters to Atticus*, 5.
[45] Caesar, *Letters to Atticus*, 5.13.

invaluable in the next century.

Caesar was also able to assess the Britons, informing Roman attitudes from that point onward. He explained, "The interior of Britain is inhabited by those of whom they say that it is handed down by tradition that they were born in the island itself. The maritime portion by those who had passed over from the country of the Belgae for the purpose of plunder and war, almost all of whom are called by the names of those states from which being sprung they went thither and having waged war continued there and began to cultivate the lands. The number of people is countless and their buildings exceedingly numerous for the most part very like those of Gaul. They do not regard it lawful to eat the hare, and the cock and the goose, they do, however, breed them for amusement and pleasure."[46]

Caesar concluded that the most civilized of the British tribes were those living in Kent, though he noted the Britons did not sow corn but tended to live on milk and flesh instead. He confirmed all of the tribes used blue woad to decorate themselves for war, wore their hair long, and used animal skins for clothing. He was intrigued by the custom of their shaving every part of their bodies except for the hair and upper lip, and even more fascinated by the practice of sharing up to a dozen wives between warriors. The father of any child born from such unions was, he recorded, always assumed to be that of the first husband.[47]

Caesar was also able to study British military tactics, and he provided details about chariot warfare, which was a specialty of the British: "Firstly they drive about in all directions and throw their weapons and generally break the ranks of the enemy with the very dread of their horses and the noise of their wheels and when they have worked themselves in between the troops of horse, leap from their chariots to engage on foot. The charioteers in the meantime withdraw some little distance from the battle and so place themselves with the chariots that if their masters are overpowered by the number of the enemy they may have a ready retreat to their own troops. Thus they display in battle the speed of horse, together with the firmness of infantry and by daily practice and exercise, attain to such expertness that they are accustomed, even on a declining and steep place to check their horses at full speed and manage and turn them in an instant and run along the pole and stand on the yoke, and thence betake themselves with the greatest celerity to their chariots again."[48]

Caesar undoubtedly respected the Britons' military attributes and even copied a style of boat he had seen on the island during the subsequent civil war he fought against Pompey years later.[49] He was less enthusiastic about the Druidic religion—which he believed originated in Britain— going so far as to claim the Druids in Gaul had all been trained there.[50] He also appreciated the

---

[46] Caesar, *Letters to Atticus*, 5.12.
[47] Caesar, *Letters to Atticus*, 5.14.
[48] Caesar, *Letters to Atticus*, 4.33.
[49] Caesar, *Letters to Atticus*, 1.54.
[50] Caesar, *Letters to Atticus*, 6.13.

economic potential of the island and was convinced it would be a valuable addition to the Roman Empire: "The number of cattle is great. They use either brass or iron rings, determined at a certain weight, as their money. Tin is produced in the midland regions in the maritime, iron…there is timber of every description."[51]

Caesar did not conquer Britain, but what he did do—especially by restoring Mandubracius to the Trinovantine throne—was begin the system of client kingdoms. In so doing, he brought the island within the Roman orbit. One of his most significant successes, although perhaps only realized retrospectively in 43 CE, was that he established alliances with key kings. Trading links also developed significantly over the coming years.

Caesar's contribution to the eventual conquest of Britain is best summed up by Tacitus: "It was, in fact, the divine Julius who first of all Romans entered Britain with an army, he overawed the natives by a successful battle and made himself master of the coast, but it may be said that he revealed, rather than bequeathed, Britain to Rome."[52]

From Caesar's second invasion in 54 BCE to Emperor Claudius's invasion nearly 100 years later, the status quo between Rome and Britain—involving hostages and tribute—was maintained without direct military occupation of the island. Caesar's presumptive heir, Octavian, prepared to invade in 34 BCE, 27 BCE, and 25 BCE, but two of these dates were abandoned due to pressing problems elsewhere in the empire and the third was preempted because the British tribes came to terms with Rome.[53]

---

[51] Caesar, *Letters to Atticus*, 5.2.
[52] Tacitus, *The Life of Cnæus Julius Agricola*, 13.
[53] Dio Cassius, *Roman History*, 49.38.

An ancient statue of Augustus

Strabo reflected on Augustus' policy toward Britain during this period, concluding it was founded on pure pragmatism: "And for the purposes of political power, there would be no advantage in knowing such distant countries and their inhabitants, particularly where the people live in islands which are such that they can neither injure or benefit us in any way, because of their isolation. For although the Romans could have possessed Britain, they scorned to do so, for they saw that there was nothing at all to fear from Britain, since they are not strong enough to cross over and attack us. No corresponding advantages would arise by taking over and holding the country. For at present more seems to accrue from the customs duties on their commerce than direct taxation could supply, if we deduct the cost of maintaining an army to garrison the island and collect the tribute. The unprofitableness of an occupation would be still more marked in the case of the other islands near Britain."[54]

---

[54] Strabo, *Geography*, 2.5.8.

The next potential invasion of Britain was led by Caligula in 40 CE, initially reported on by Suetonius and then Dio Cassius, who recounted the story of Caligula collecting huge amounts of sea shells and declaring this the tribute he had won from Neptune. "Having secured these spoils for it was evident that he needed booty for his triumphal procession, he became greatly elated, as if he had subdued the Ocean itself. He gave many presents to his soldiers. He took back the shells to Rome in order to exhibit his booty there as well."[55]

Louis le Grand's picture of a bust of Caligula

By 40 CE, the political situation in Britain was in turmoil due to the emergence of the Catevellauni as the most powerful tribe. They displaced Rome's allies, the Trinovantes, which prompted Rome to consider invasion. It is not known what made Caligula decide to abandon his invasion plans, though he certainly took steps that aided Claudius three years later. Most notably, it was under Caligula that the Romans built a lighthouse at what is now Boulogne, a structure that stood until the 16th century.

Dio Cassius wrote extensively on the real invasion, which began in 43 CE. From his work, it is known that the invasion force was led by Aulus Plautius, the distinguished senator, and

---

[55] Dio Cassius, *Roman History*, 59, 25.1.3.

comprised four legions, one of which was commanded by Vespasian, the future emperor. The army assembled at Boulogne, crossing over to Britain in three phases and apparently landing at Richborough on the east coast of Kent. Richborough had a large, natural harbor, and excavations do seem to confirm this was the landing place. That said, some historians argue the landing place was in the vicinity of Noviomagus, Chichester, in territory formerly ruled by Verica. Ostensibly, the invasion had taken place to restore Verica as ruler.[56]

British resistance to the Romans was more organized than in the time of Caesar and was led by two formidable commanders, Togodumnus and Caratacus, son of Cunobeline, King of the Catevellauni. The two armies met near Rochester on the River Medway, and after two days of intense fighting, the Romans emerged victorious. The Britons retreated to the Thames, where Togodumnus was killed. Caratacus evaded capture, however, and fled to the west to continue his resistance against the Romans.

Aulus Plautius was, he believed, assured of victory and sent for Claudius to join him for the final push. Dio Cassius claimed Aulus Plautius sent for Claudius because he needed the emperor to secure the victory: "On receiving his message Claudius committed affairs in Rome including the command of the troops to his fellow consul Lucius Vitellius, whom he had kept in office, like himself, for the full half year and set out for Britain...Taking over the command of the troops in Britain himself he crossed the Thames and engaged the barbarians who had assembled to oppose him. He defeated them and captured Camulodunum, the capital of Cunobelinus. After this he won over a number of tribes some by diplomacy some by force and was saluted as Imperator several times, contrary to precedent."[57]

Claudius was certainly no military man, and on his triumphal arch in Rome, it is claimed that Claudius received the surrender of 11 kings without any losses. In *Twelve Caesars*, Suetonius states that Claudius received the surrender of the Britons without battle or bloodshed.[58] It is more likely that by the time Claudius arrived, the Britons had, in effect, been beaten, so the elephants and heavy war engines brought by Claudius were superfluous. They would, however, have presented an imposing spectacle for Claudius's march to Camulodunum, where the Romans had established their new capital.

Despite having had very little to do with the actual defeat of the Britons, Claudius milked the victory for all it was worth. Dio Cassius noted, "The Senate on hearing of his achievements voted him the title Britannicus, and gave him permission to hold a triumph. They also voted an annual festival to commemorate the event and decreed that two triumphal arches should be erected, one in Rome and one in Gaul, since it was from Gaul that he had crossed over into Britain. They bestowed on his son the same title and indeed in a way Britannicus came to be the

---

[56] Strabo, *Geography*, 4.5.2.
[57] Dio Cassius, *Roman History*, 60.19.1-21.5.
[58] Suetonius, *Life of Claudius*, 17.

boy's usual name."[59]

Marie-Lan Nguyen's picture of a bust of Claudius

Vespasian pursued Caratacus west and set up a legionary base at Exeter. While this was going on, the Legio IX was sent north and established a Roman center at Lincoln.

Josephus seemingly exaggerated Vespasian's role in the conquest of Britain, claiming it had been he who had added Britain to the Empire, "and thus provided Claudius, the father of Nero, with a triumph which cost him no personal exertion."[60] Regardless of whoever was most responsible, within only four years of the invasion, the area south of a line from the Humber to the Severn estuary was under Roman control.

Roman consolidation of their new province continued apace under the new Governor Publius Ostorius Scapula who, in 47 CE, began a campaign against the Welsh tribes.

Key to the Roman success was their defeat of Caratacus whom they bested in the Battle of

---

[59] Dio Cassius, *Roman History*, 60.22.1-23.6.
[60] Josephus, *The Wars of the Jews*, 3.1.2(4).

Caer Caradoc. He sought sanctuary with the Brigantes, whose queen, Cartimandua, promptly handed him over to her Roman allies. His wife and daughter were already in Roman hands, having been captured after the battle. Tacitus described Caratacus in fairly glowing terms, writing, "The natural ferocity of the inhabitants was intensified by their belief in the prowess of Caratacus whose many undefeated battles and even many victories had made him pre-eminent among British chieftains. His deficiency in strength was compensated by superior cunning and topographical knowledge. Transferring the war to the country of the Ordovices he was joined by everyone who found the prospect of a Roman peace alarming."[61]

Tacitus recalls that Caratacus was held in some esteem in Rome despite nine years of warfare, and although he was paraded through Rome as a prisoner, Claudius pardoned his erstwhile foe after he had made a noble speech to the Senate. He may have lived the remainder of his life in the city.

The defeat of Caratacus was not, however, the end of the disturbances in Britain, and further trouble erupted with the Silures and the Brigantes. Ostorius died shortly after Caratacus's defeat and was succeeded by Aulus Didius Gallus, who, upon his arrival in Britain, found that a Roman brigade under Manlius Valens had suffered a reversal. The whole incident was magnified, for various reasons, by both sides in an internal struggle between Brigantine factions. Having resolved that issue, Gallus turned his attention to the consolidation of Roman gains in Wales. Nero became Emperor in 54 CE, and he was keen to expand the invasion even further north. He appointed Quintus Veranius as governor, and he and his successor, Gaius Suetonius Paulinus, extended Roman control in Wales, destroying the seat of Druidical power on Mona, present-day Anglesey, in 60 CE.

The Romans seem to have had an almost pathological hatred of the Druids since the days of Julius Caesar, and this sentiment was shared by Claudius. It was the determination to exterminate them that led to a significant part of the Roman forces in Britain being in the north when the Iceni revolt erupted.

The final subjugation of Wales and the suppression of the Druids had to be deferred in 60 CE because the Romans had to turn their attention to the biggest threat to their invasion since 43 CE: the Revolt of the Iceni.

While the death of Prasutagus and the subsequent treatment of his wife and daughters was undoubtedly a major factor in the Iceni rebellion, the whole uprising had more deep-seated causes. Tacitus recorded, "Prasutagus, King of the Iceni, after a life of long and renowned prosperity, had made the emperor co-heir with his own two daughters. Prasutagus hoped by this submissiveness to reserve his kingdom and household from attack. But it turned out otherwise. After his death, the kingdom and household alike were plundered like prizes of war, the one by

---

[61] Tacitus, *The Annals*, 12.31-3.

Roman officers the other by Roman slaves. As a beginning his widow Boudicca was flogged and their daughters raped. The Icenian chiefs were deprived of their hereditary estates as if the Romans had been given the whole country. The king's own relatives were treated like slaves and the humiliated Iceni feared still worse now that they had been reduced to provincial status. So they rebelled."[62]

The Iceni had rebelled in 47 BCE, and it appears that Prasutagus had been put onto the throne by the Romans as a way of keeping control of the area. Prasutagus's will omitted Boudicca—contrary to normal Celtic practice—which has been assumed by some historians to be because of her open hostility to Rome. The terms of his will, it is suggested, were constructed in such a way as to help his daughters continue his policy of cooperation with Rome and thereby sideline Boudicca.[63]

Whether Boudicca was a long-standing opponent of Rome or not, she certainly seized the opportunity—presented by her own ill-treatment and that of her daughters—to begin another revolt against the Romans. The trouble quickly spread to the Trinovantes, who had their own grievances against Rome. Britons felt generally angry at the establishment of Rome's imperial cult, which was, of course, specifically intended to impress the natives with the might and majesty of both Rome and the emperor, as well as to act as the focal point for loyalty. The Romans used the cult in a number of ways, including enrolling the local aristocracy as priests, thus involving them in Roman public life. The intention was to Romanize the class of natives that would become the governing class, and who would then undertake the burden of running and administering the province in Rome's interests.

The attempt misfired badly, and the spark of rebellion created by Boudicca's treatment quickly lit fires elsewhere. Dio Cassius, however, put forward an alternative explanation for the outbreak of the revolt: "Claudius had given sums of money to the leading Britons and according to Catus Decianus, the procurator of the island, the money had to be returned together the rest. The confiscation of this money was the pretext for war. In addition, Seneca, with a view to a good rate of interest, had lent the reluctant islanders 40,000,000 sesterces and had then called it all in at once and not very gently. So rebellion broke out."[64]

As well as resentment about the collection of money, Cassius Dio blamed Boudicca for the rebellion, and his description of her atrocities against the Romans is both graphic and damning. She first struck at Camulodunum, where she massacred the entire population and razed the settlement to the ground. Suetonius was busily engaged in Mona and could not help. The Ninth Roman Division, led by Rufus, marched to aid the settlement but was routed by the Iceni. Suetonius marched south to defend Londinium, but upon reaching the city, he decided his forces

---

[62] Tacitus, *The Annals*, 14.31.
[63] *Boudica Britannia; Rebel War Leader and Queen* by Aldhouse-Green (2006). Harlow, Pearson Longman.
[64] Dio Cassius, *Roman History*, 62.2.1-4.

could not match the rebels, so he left it to its fate. "He decided to sacrifice the one town to save the general situation. Undeflected by the tears and prayers of those who begged for his help he gave the signal to move, taking into his company any who could join it. Those who were unfit for war because of their sex, or too aged to go or too fond of the place to leave were butchered by the enemy."[65]

Having taken Londinium, the rebels quickly moved on to Verulamium, where the massacres continued. "The same massacre continued at Verulamium, for the barbarian British, happiest when looting and unenthusiastic about real effort, bypassed the forts and garrisons and headed for where they knew lay the maximum of undefended booty. Something like 70,000 Roman citizens and other friends of Rome died in the places I have mentioned; the Britons took no prisoners sold no captives as slaves and went in for none of the usual trading of war. They wasted no time in getting down to the bloody business of hanging, burning and crucifying. It was as if they feared that retribution might catch up [to] them while their vengeance was only half complete."[66]

While the Britons were busy destroying Verulamium, Suetonius was scouting out the best possible site for a decisive battle. He chose a place where his troops would not be subjected to ambush and settled in to wait for the Britons, who duly arrived in huge numbers. Their confidence in victory was such that they brought their wives and children with them and left them in carts stationed at the edge of the battlefield.[67] Both leaders are said to have inspired their troops with rousing speeches before Suetonius gave the signal for the battle to commence.

His infantry moved forward, throwing their javelins, and Boudicca's superior numbers gave her no advantage in the narrow battlefield the Romans had chosen. Indeed, the vast throng impeded each other, providing easy targets for the Romans. The rebels were forced back, and the Romans advanced in their famous wedge formation, easily cutting through the enemies' lines. As Suetonius ordered in his cavalry and auxiliaries to press home his advantage, the Britons turned to flee. The carts they had arranged around the battlefield slowed their retreat, and the rout turned into an absolute massacre. Tacitus wrote that "the remaining Britons fled with difficulty since their ring of wagons blocked the outlets. The Romans did not spare even the women. Baggage animals too, transfixed with weapons added to the heaps of dead."[68] Boudicca and her daughters escaped, but it is thought they later committed suicide.

---

[65] Tacitus, *The Annals*, 14.33.
[66] Tacitus, *The Annals*, 14.33.
[67] Tacitus, *The Annals*, 14.33.
[68] Tacitus, *The Annals*, 14.33.

A. Brady's picture of a statue depicting Boudicca in her chariot before the battle

The location of the Battle of Watling Street is still unknown today. Theories range from King's Cross in London to Church Stowe in Northampton. Whatever the case, Boudicca's defeat was followed by a program of severe suppression of the indigenous population, initiated by Suetonius. Indeed, the measures he introduced to pacify Britain were so severe that he was eventually recalled to Rome and replaced by Publius Petronius Turpilianus, who tried a gentler approach to pacification. Neither approach proved entirely successful, and sporadic revolts continued to break out until Agricola put a definitive end to any hope the Britons had of expelling their conquerors.

Agricola

The first known written mention of any contact between Rome and Scotland is in the record of the British kings who formally submitted to Emperor Claudius at Colchester in 43 CE.[69] 11 kings attended, one of whom was the King of Orkney. Claudius's invasion had taken place only three months before this meeting. Despite the lack of written records, given the distance from Orkney to Colchester, it must be assumed that this king had been in contact prior to the campaign to practically have been able to be in attendance (although the submission does appear out of character, given the vehement opposition mounted by the Caledonians to Roman incursions, and the basis of Orkney's apparent weak resistance is a mystery).

---

[69] P. 172-173, *Before Scotland: The Story of Scotland Before History* by Moffat, A. (2005). London. Thames & Hudson. See also; p. 5, *The New History of Orkney* by Thomson, W. P. L. (2008). Edinburgh. Birlinn

For the next 40 years little is known in terms of the continuing contact between the Romans and the Caledonians, and it is only when Agricola arrives on the scene that direct prolonged conflict occurs. Gnaeus Julius Agricola was born in 40 CE in Frejus, in what is now southern France, into a senatorial family. He is best known for being the military mastermind who oversaw the Roman conquest of Britain, with most of the details of his career coming from a biography *De vita et moribus Iulii Agricolae ("*On the life and character of Julius Agricola"), written by his son-in-law, the Roman historian Tacitus, in 98 CE. Agricola's early military career was spent in Britain where he initially served as *tribunus militum* to the Governor Suetonius Paulinus (58 CE – 62 CE), meaning that he was in Britain at the time of Boudicca's[70] famous rebellion in 60 CE He went on to be *quaestor* (64 A.D), tribune of the people (66 CE), praetor (68 CE), and then in 71 CE he was made commander of the 20th Legion in Britain. His career continued to go well, and after spells as Governor of Aquitania, he became a consul in 77 CE He finally returned to Britain in 78 CE as governor.

---

[70] Boudicca was Queen of the Iceni tribe.

A statue of Agricola

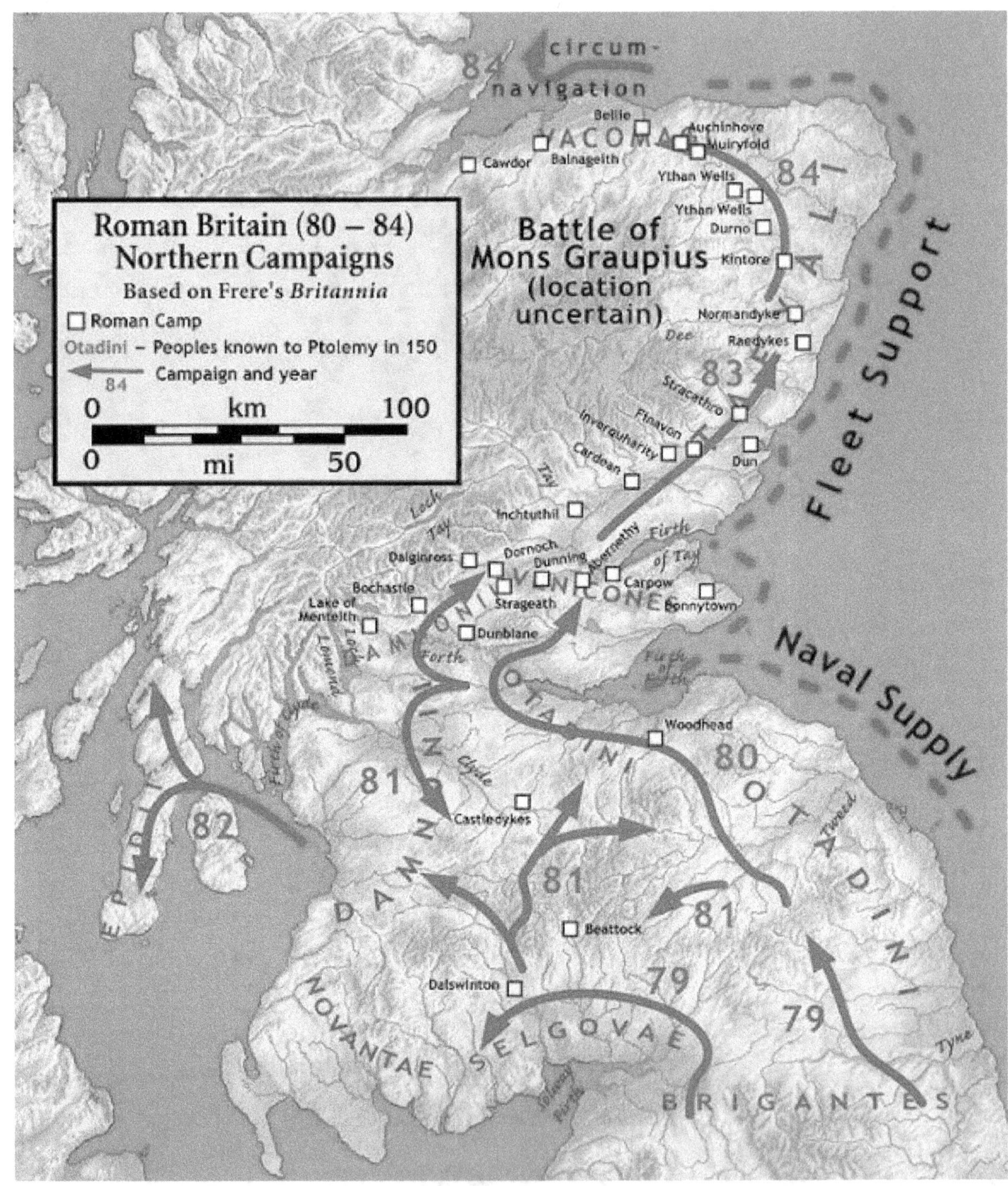

A map of Roman campaigns and conquests in Britain during the time of Agricola

In an assessment of Agricola as a governor, accounts seem to depict him as being skilled as a military commander and a just administrator who won the respect of the local population.[71] He extended Roman authority northwards, and by doing so inevitably came into contact with the

[71] Tacitus, *Agricola*, LIV-LV, LIX, LXXVII. See also; p. 19, 21-22, *Tacitus, Vol. I* by Syme, R. (1958). Oxford. Oxford University Press.

Caledonians. By the time of Pliny the Elder (23/24 CE – 79 CE), Roman knowledge of the geography of Scotland had extended to include the Hebudes, the Hebrides, Dumna, the Outer Hebrides, the Caledonian Forest, and the Caledonians. Agricola sent a fleet to survey and map the Scottish coastline in 79 CE, and this was followed by an advance into Caledonia in stages during 80 CE and 81 CE. By 83 CE, Agricola was able to secure southern Scotland despite what Tacitus describes as "armed resistance on a large scale".[72]

As soon as his troops had established a foothold in southern Scotland, Agricola ordered the building of a large fort at Trimontium, near Melrose, in what is today the Scottish Borders. Archaeologists have discovered the foundations of several successive structures reflecting the history of the fort that was garrisoned and abandoned several times during the coming centuries. Agricola then forced his way northwards to the River Tay, where he established a number of forts, including a major legionary fortress at Inchtuthil.

The total size of the Roman garrison in Scotland during the Flavian period (80 A.D – 96 CE) was somewhere in the region of 25,000 troops. Such a force required approximately 20,000 tons of grain per annum, and so the logistical problems surrounding supply were always difficult. Similarly, providing the materials needed to construct the forts Agricola demanded presented major practical issues. It has been estimated that the Romans used 1 million cubic feet of timber during the 1st century CE alone.[73] At the incomplete Inchtuthil site, 10 tons of nails were discovered by archaeologists, giving an indication of the scale of the project. This fort had a garrison of 6,000 men and used 30 kilometers of wood for the walls alone.

The Caledonians recognized that they were not in a position to meet the highly disciplined Roman troops in a head-on battle and so resorted to guerrilla tactics. They targeted their attacks against the individual smaller Roman forts and any small groups of troops that wandered too far from larger units. They were quick to seize any opportunity the Romans gave them to inflict casualties and on one occasion would have totally wiped out the 9th Legion in a surprise attack if Agricola's cavalry had not arrived in time[74].

By the summer of 84 CE, Agricola and his legions had moved into north-east Scotland, and at last his enemies decided to confront him in a pitched battle. Tacitus says the site of the battle was at Mons Graupius,[75] somewhere in the Grampian Mountains, but provides few other details about the precise location (and the site has still not been conclusively identified). Why the Caledonians abandoned their guerrilla warfare tactics for this battle is unclear, but it proved to be a disastrous decision. S. Frere suggests one reason was because Agricola had sent his fleet to

---

[72] Ibid.

[73] P. 206, "The Roman Presence: Brief Interludes" by Hanson, W. S (2003). In: Edwards, K. J. & Ralston, I. B.M. (eds) *Scotland After the Ice Age: Environment, Archaeology and History, 8000 BC – AD 1000*. Edinburgh. Edinburgh University Press.

[74] Tacitus, *Agricola*, XXXVII. See also; P. 42, *Tacitus – Agricola, Germany, and Dialogue on Orators* by H.W. Benario (2006). Hackett Publishing.

[75] Tacitus, *Agricola*, XXIX.

burn the Caledonians' supply areas. This action created a stark choice: react or be starved into submission.[76]

Tacitus estimated that the Caledonians were able to field an army of 30,000 under Calgacus,[77] while the Romans had a force of 15,000. Calgacus was the first Caledonian to be recorded in history but only by Tacitus, who says of him that he was "the most distinguished for birth and valour among the chieftains".[78] Tacitus wrote a speech which he attributes to Calgacus. While it is more than likely totally made up,[79] it does, however, sum up what the Caledonians probably thought of the Roman invaders: "To all of us slavery is a thing unknown; there are no lands beyond us, and even the sea is not safe, menaced as we are by a Roman fleet. And thus in war and battle, in which the brave find glory, even the coward will find safety. […] Romans are the robbers of the world, having by their universal plunder exhausted the land, they rifle the deep. If the enemy be rich, they are rapacious; if he be poor, they lust for dominion; neither the east nor the west has been able to satisfy them. Alone among men they covet with equal eagerness poverty and riches. To robbery, slaughter, plunder, they give the lying name of empire; they make a solitude and call it peace".[80]

The figure given by Tacitus for the Caledonian army seems far too high considering the population at the time and the losses they had already suffered. However, it is not surprising that Tacitus would have wanted to make the victory as heroic as possible. He claims that the Caledonians had the advantage of the higher ground in the battle, but in spite of this, it was Roman tactics and experience that won out. The Romans used their short stabbing sword, the *gladius*, in close quarter combat, which proved particularly formidable against the unpointed swords used by the tribesmen, which they could not use in their normal fashion in this type of battle.

Auxiliary troops from Germany, Holland, and Belgium made up the front line, while the veterans took up the rear. During a long period of hand-to-hand fighting, at one point the Caledonians outflanked the Romans, which might have proved decisive if, once again, the Roman cavalry had not intervened to push the tribesmen back. Tacitus gives some details of the battle: "The Britons, armed with long swords and short targets, with steadiness and dexterity avoided or struck down our missile weapons, and at the same time poured in a torrent of their own".[81] Agricola changed his tactics and "encouraged three Batavian and two Tungrian cohorts to fall in and come to close quarters; a method of fighting familiar to these veteran soldiers"; this proved decisive as "the enormous British swords, blunt at the point, are unfit for close grappling,

---

[76] P. 111, *Britannia: A History of Roman Britain* by S.S. Frere (1987). Routledge: London

[77] Also referred to as Calgacos or Galgacus.

[78] Tacitus, *Agricola*, XXVIIII.

[79] There are several reasons historians doubt its authenticity; Tacitus's father-in-law was Agricola; Calgacus is not mentioned again, before or during the battle, nor is he included in the list of hostages after the battle; no other source mentions a chieftain with this name.

[80] Tacitus, *Agricola*, XXX.

[81] Ibid, XXXVI.

and engaging in a confined space".[82] The Roman infantry and cavalry then combined to rout the Caledonians. Tacitus estimates that 10,000 Caledonians were killed.

As already stated, the exact location of the battle is unknown, with 29 sites having been identified as credible possibilities. The most recent suggestion comes from an article in the *Herald Scotland* (2013, May), citing a professor from the University of Navarre in Pamplona, who concluded that the battle took place at Bennachie by Inverurie in Aberdeenshire. Professor Breeze argues "that the words 'Mons Graupius' relate to Welsh 'crib' (ridge), and the actual shape of Bennachie provides confirmation of this etymology".[83] The general surrounding area was remote, and those who managed to survive disappeared into the mountains, where they immediately returned to their guerrilla tactics and added a scorched earth policy of burning their own homes and farms. Tacitus claims they even murdered their own wives to prevent them being captured by the Romans.[84]

On the day following the battle, Tacitus explained that "the hills were deserted, houses smoking in the distance, and our scouts did not meet a soul,"[85] and the Romans clearly had no doubt that Agricola's victory was a huge success. Modern assessments of the effects of the battle, however, are not quite as positive: "Tacitus described Mons Graupius as a great Roman victory; who can blame him. But was it? The fact remains that Agricola retired southwards when it was over. Moreover, when he left Britain a few months later, the frontier between the Romans and the Caledonians was nowhere near the site of the battle. It was more than 150 miles south, and over the years that followed, the Roman occupation of Scotland contracted and contracted. It probably never consisted of more than the holding of key forts and fortlets, and as time went by less and less of them".[86]

Nevertheless, the victory certainly meant Agricola had, for the moment, complete control of Scotland, and he may have completed his total physical conquest if it was not for the fact that his plans were thwarted by his recall to Rome by the Emperor Domitian (r. 81-96 CE) who wanted the general to come back and defend the strategically more important Danube frontier.

Indeed, the value to the Romans of the Battle of Mons Graupius in the end was negligible to the Roman Empire. It did have a lasting impact on the Caledonians though, who learned from their defeat and never engaged the Romans again in a major pitched battle. This decision to

---

[82] Ibid.

[83] 'Study reveals Bennachie could be location of Mons Graupius' by A. Breeze (2013, May 21). The Herald. [ONLINE] Available at: https://www.heraldscotland.com/opinion/13105640.study-reveals-bennachie-could-be-location-of-mons-graupius/. See also; 'Philology on Tacitus's Graupian Hill and Trucculan Harbour' by A. Breeze (2002). Proceedings of the Society of Antiquaries of Scotland Vol. 132, pp.305-311.

[84] Tacitus, *Agricola*, XXXVIII.
[85] Ibid, XXXIX.
[86] P. 23, *The History of* Scotland by P. Somerset Fry & S. Somerset Fry (1982). London: Routledge.

revert to guerrilla tactics proved decisive in preventing the Romans from establishing a permanent presence in Scotland, and McHardy summed up Rome's failure: "The Roman conquest of Europe had relied on the organised and regular disposition of highly disciplined legions, numbering in thousands of men each, and here they were in a terrain in which the deployment of such troops was highly problematic. On the other hand, the small groups of native warriors, trained in raiding within the environment, would have no problems in using their own military skills in any situation where the Romans were exposed. The hit-and-run tactics of modern guerrilla warfare serves well as a model for attempting to understand how the indigenous peoples surely resisted the might of the Roman armies".[87]

It is not known how far north Agricola had managed to advance before his return to Rome but recent discoveries in Easter Ross and the uncovering of temporary campsites near Portmahomack in 1949, in conjunction with a site discovered in 1991 at Tarradale on the Black Isle near the Beauly Firth that conforms to the morphology of a Roman camp or fort, suggest that he went further into the north of Scotland than previously thought. It may be that as the Romans advanced, the tribesmen re-occupied hill forts such as Dun Mor in Perthshire and constructed new ones in the northeast, such as Hill O'Christ's Kirk in Aberdeenshire, in an effort to counter the invasion. Archaeology has also uncovered a series of fortlets and signal stations, known as the Gask Ridge, constructed from the River Teith at Doune, near Stirling, to what is now the city of Perth on the Tay. These small forts were linked to the Glen Forts of Fendoch, Dalginross, Bochastle, Malling and Drumquassle. This border, however, had already been abandoned by 86 CE.

Whether Agricola could have coped with the type of warfare re-embarked on by the natives and emerged victorious is a moot point, but his recall by the emperor proved to be an unlooked-for reprieve for the Caledonians. In the coming years, the constant raids by the Caledonians resulted in the Romans slowly retreating southwards to a line between the Rivers Forth and Clyde, and Emperor Trajan was responsible for most of the withdrawals from the area during his reign (98 CE – 117 A.D). In the 40 years after Agricola's victory, there are no literary sources that mention Scotland, and it was during this period that the IXth Legion based at York was "lost". While legend and fictional accounts suggest that it mysteriously disappeared on a campaign in Caledonia, it is more likely that it was withdrawn from Britain as part of Trajan's restructuring of the empire's defenses and was disbanded at some point after that. The gradual withdrawal southwards continued, and by the end of Trajan's reign in 117 CE, the new northern border had been established on a line between the Solway and the Tyne. The Romans were never able to re-establish full control over southern Scotland, although there were attempts to do so.

---

[87]Chapter 2, *A New History of the* Picts by S. McHardy (2010). Chippenham: CPI Antony Rowe.

Hadrian's Wall

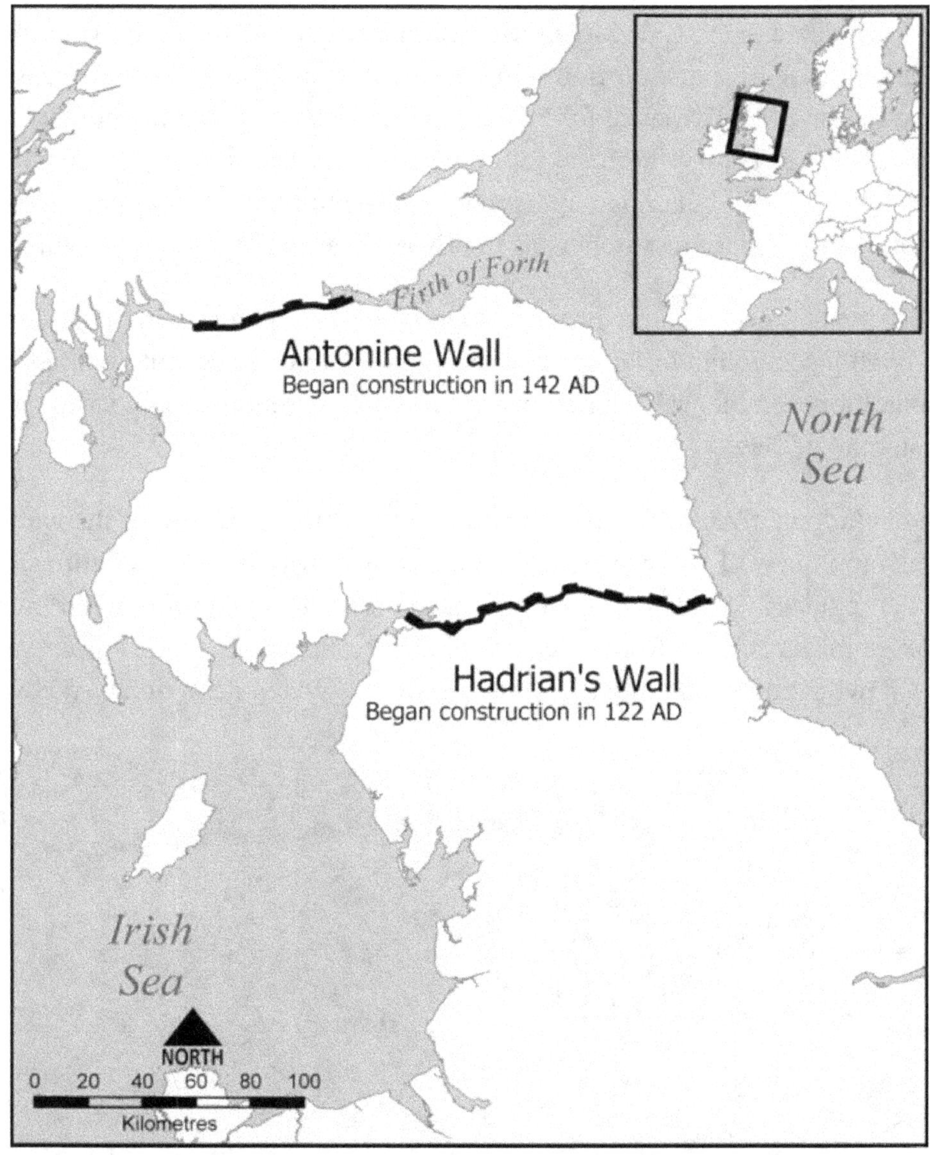

Construction of Hadrian's Wall began in 122 at Newcastle (*Pons Aelius*) and went all the way to Bowness-on-Solway. The line ran parallel to the old Stanegate military road but was as much as two miles north of it in places. This was a strategic decision, for the Stanegate, being a road, ran through valleys and other flat areas for ease of movement, but a wall is at its strongest when it's atop a commanding position that inhibits attackers and allows defenders to see farther. By moving slightly to the north, the wall could be positioned on the hills to the north of the valleys through which the Stanegate ran, and the portion of the wall at the center of the island could take advantage of a series of rough crags, which at times have sheer, north-facing cliffs.

Much of the barrier was 10 feet thick and made of stone bonded with puddled clay, though in other places, the wall is only 7 feet thick. While the thinner portion of the wall seems unduly weak, it must be remembered that the Caledonians did not have any siege equipment, so even though the wall would have been easy enough for a well-equipped Roman army to pierce, it must have seemed formidable to the Caledonian tribes. In fact, it seems the entire wall was originally intended to be 10 feet thick, but a portion of it was made thinner in order to decrease costs and speed up construction time. Evidence for this can be seen in some architectural details, such as at Milecastle 48 at Poltross Burn, where the fortlet (small fort) was constructed in such a way as to accommodate a thicker wall but ended up having only the thinner wall connected to it. The two portions are known to modern researchers as the Broad Wall and the Narrow Wall.

Most of the stone is limestone, the most common type of stone found in the region. The facing stones were roughly squared in order to fit better into regular courses, but no attempt was made at fine dressing. Stones in the wall's interior were rougher, essentially comprising a rubble fill with a large amount of clay.

No portion of Hadrian's Wall has survived to its top, so reconstruction of the wall is theoretical, but atop the wall was probably a protected walkway with crenellations, toothlike slabs of stone at regular intervals with bare spaces in between, a pattern familiar on medieval castles. Evidence for this comes from similar walls from other parts of the empire, as well as the Rudge Cup, a bowl dating from around 150 that shows a stylized depiction of the wall.

The Rudge Cup

The wall stretched westwards 80 Roman miles to Bowness-on-Solway, 15.5 miles (25 km) west of the modern city of Carlisle, which in Roman times was called Luguvalium. Between the

River Irthing and Bowness-on-Solway, the wall was made of turf and timber instead of stone, but the towers continued to be of stone. West of Bowness-on-Solway, the wall stopped, but the milecastles and towers continued in their regular pattern for at least another 26 miles (42 km) along the coast. Doubtless this was to watch for sea raiders, like the later Saxon Shore forts along the southeast coast of Britannia.

Remains of the wall at Milecastle 39

In front of the wall was a ditch, placed several paces to the north of the wall so as not to cause erosion of the wall itself, and it was cut along standard Roman military lines in a steep V shape about 30-40 feet wide at the top and almost 10 feet deep. The excavated earth wasn't used to make a rampart (as was common with an earthen defense system) but was instead formed into a broad mound to the north of the ditch, higher at the south end than the north but with all parts clearly visible from the top of the wall. This ancient tactic, known as a *glacis*, created a clear "killing zone" where attackers could find no cover.

At times, the wall was able to take advantage of natural features to make some portions all but impregnable. In the central portion are numerous crags that rise steeply up from the surrounding ground. The wall goes right up and over them, and one section several miles long actually follows a sheer cliff. Moreover, the wall was strengthened at regular intervals by towers and forts and backed by a broad ditch on the south side called the *Vallum*, which is discussed further below.

Running between and parallel to the wall and the *Vallum* was the Military Way, a replacement for the Stanegate. It ran along the entire length of the wall from the Tyne to Solway Firth and had branch roads leading to forts and settlements. It was similar to many Roman roads, being 18-20 Roman feet wide (18-19.5 modern feet), and had a gravel foundation with curb stones to resist erosion. Atop the foundation was a layer of small basalt stones, and atop this was a surface of fine gravel. This major addition to the wall came at the time of the reoccupation after the abandonment of the Antonine Wall in the late second century.

The material required for building Hadrian's Wall is staggering. Some 1.5 million tons of stone, much of it dressed, was required to build the wall, turrets, milecastles, and forts. This required 15,500 tons of lime and 53,500 pounds of sand for mortar, plus 3,000 tons of water to mix it. Another 198,500 tons of clay was needed for the core. The building work was done by the legions and auxiliary units themselves, which was a common practice that both saved money and stationed soldiers at a vulnerable location until it could be fortified. Much of a Roman legionnaire's life was spent building, not fighting, and thousands of inscriptions have come down from the Roman world of one legion or another proclaiming they had built a fort or a bridge or a stretch of road. Inscriptions show that three legions—the *XX Valeria Victrix* from Chesters, the *II Augusta* from Caerleon, and the *VI Victrix pia fidelis* from York—worked on the wall, along with detachments from the navy (*classis Britannia*) and various auxiliary units. For example, a fragmentary inscription from Milecastle 50 reads, "From the Second Legion Augusta, the Seventh Cohort under the charge of..." Sadly, the name of the soldier/overseer has been lost to history.

Men often brought construction skills from their civilian life into practice when they joined the army, so carpenters, stonemasons, tile makers, potters, thatchers, and other such professions were valued when searching for recruits. On top of that, local civilians or civilian work crews may have been brought in from elsewhere to help, but there is no direct evidence for this. The building of the wall was overseen by the Governor of Britannia, Aulus Platorius Nepos, who replaced Falco in 122, and several inscriptions found along the wall mention his name.

The entire defensive system was completed before Hadrian's death, a testament to Roman ingenuity and resourcefulness and a project that cemented Hadrian's reputation as one of the empire's great builders.

Hadrian's Wall initially proved successful in providing the conditions to enable commerce to flourish in northern Britain, and the stability it gave led to a burgeoning economy in the region. This resulted in a much speedier Romanisation of the province of Britain than would otherwise have been the case, and led to the growth of towns and cities, and to increased individual prosperity that manifested itself in larger and more luxurious homes for the wealthy.

Scotland was not entirely forgotten, however, and the constant fear of, or actual, raids may have led Emperor Antoninus Pius to order his general Quintus Lollius Urbicus, whom he promoted as Governor of Britain in 138, to try once again to subdue southern Scotland. The campaign was initially successful, and a new frontier was established by building what became known as the Antonine Wall on a line from the Forth to the Clyde. This wall was built of turf with a fronting ditch and ran for 37 miles. It was a much less elaborate, or effective, structure than Hadrian's Wall but was built on the same basic principles, with forts placed strategically and smaller stations established between them.

There is little in the sources to explain why there was this attempt to re-establish the frontier further north. Security concerns are the most likely explanation, although it may have been built for propaganda purposes to demonstrate that the empire was expanding. Presumably, however, the further the "savages" could be kept from the newly civilised centres in the north of England, the more the Romans would have liked it. A shorter frontier was also easier to defend, and allowed Roman troops to be concentrated more effectively. Attempts to Romanise the re-conquered area proved futile though, and numerous small revolts and a major one took place in the 150s The Romans successfully dealt with these insurrections in a military sense, but possibly realising that any attempt to bring the area under total control was going to cost too much in time, money and effort, the Antonine Wall was finally abandoned in 163.

The period of re-occupation is confused, and few details survive as to what occurred in those years in the area. More is known of a major offensive launched by a confederation of tribes in 180 during the reign of Emperor Commodus (180 [88] – 192). The tribesmen poured over Hadrian's Wall and ransacked the north of England. The Roman defences were overrun, and a Roman force totally destroyed. This was a major humiliation for the Romans, who responded in 184 by sending a punitive expedition which ravaged southern Scotland in retaliation. However, they then withdrew behind Hadrian's Wall after signing new peace treaties with the tribes. The fact that such a formal agreement could be made indicates that the tribes were perfectly capable of acting in a coordinated way, despite the large number of separate tribes and chieftains.

After the assassination of Emperor Commodus in 192, the Governor of Britain, Clodius Albinus, challenged Septimus Severus for the imperial throne and withdrew troops from Hadrian's Wall to invade Gaul in 196. He was defeated the following year and committed suicide, but according to Cassius Dio, that decision to weaken the frontier prompted the Caledonians to once again try their luck at breaching the Roman defenses to loot northern England. He wrote that the Maeatae and the Brigantes joined with the Caledonians, who, in taking part in the attack, were of course breaking the treaties they had made in 184.[89] The Maeatae were a confederation of tribes who lived somewhere north of the Antonine Wall. The historical sources are vague as to the exact region, but the area around modern-day Stirling is the most likely site.

---

[88] Commodus ruled jointly with his father, Emperor Marcus Aurelius, from 176 A.D. until his death in 180 A.D. After that, Commodus continued as the sole imperial power.
[89] Cassius Dio, *Roman History*, LXXVII, 12.

Cassius Dio wrote that the Maeatae lived between the wall and the Caledonians, but it is not clear to which wall he is referring.[90] Alexander del Mar says the identity of the Maeatae remains a mystery, but they may have been Norwegian.[91] Their confederation seems to have come together as a result of treaties made between the Romans and the frontier tribes from 184 onwards when negotiations were underway. Emperor Severus (r. 193 – 211) initiated a large-scale programme of repair of Hadrian's Wall and linked fortifications. In 208 he came to Britain with his sons and wife, determined to personally launch a new punitive expedition into Scotland and establish Roman rule in Caledonia once and for all.

Scotland in the 3rd and 4th Centuries

Severus led the campaign in 209, and both Herodian[92] and Cassius Dio refer to the Caledonians surrendering to the Emperor and ceding territory. Cassius Dio claims that the Romans suffered casualties numbering in excess of 50,000, a massive loss that he attributed to the guerrilla warfare tactics employed by the tribesmen.[93] One possibility for such severe action is that Severus's main aim for the campaign was to destroy the agricultural base of the south of Scotland, and by so doing effectively led to the genocide of the Caledonians by starvation. In the medium term that may actually have been the major result of the expedition. In the short term, however, the Caledonians re-formed their alliance with the Maeatae, and together they embarked on yet another retaliatory attack on the north of England.

Severus did not waver in his determination to slaughter all the tribesmen in southern Scotland and bring it under Roman rule. Cassius Dio recorded him as saying: "Let no one escape sheer destruction. No one our hands, not even the babe in the womb of the mother. If it be male; let it nevertheless not escape sheer destruction".[94] However, he fell ill, and before he died, passed the task on to his son Caracalla.[95] While Caracalla was carrying out his father's wishes in Scotland, Severus died at Eboracum, modern-day York, in 211. After his father's death, Caracalla's focus was now on securing the throne for himself; when his troops refused to recognize him as emperor he had to make peace with the Caledonians and retreat south of Hadrian's Wall.

In assessing Caracalla's actions, however, Frere rejects the widely held notion that Caracalla beat a hasty retreat from Scotland on hearing of his father's death and argues, rather, that he brought the campaign to a successful conclusion before the end of 211 and then returned to Rome. He cites as evidence an inscription from the large Roman fort at Carpow, which was not set up before 212 and proves, he claims, that evacuation did not even follow Caracalla's return to

---

[90] Ibid.

[91] P. 41, *'Ancient Britain in the light of modern archaeological discoveries;* by Del Mar, A. (1900). In: *The Cambridge Encyclopaedia.* [ONLINE] Available at: https://archive.org/stream/ancientbritainin01delm#page/41/mode/1up

[92] Herodian, *History of the Roman Empire*, III.14.

[93] Cassius Dio, *Roman History*, LXXVII, 13,2.

[94] Ibid, 15.1

[95] Ibid, 15,2.

Rome.[96] The inscription refers to the Legio II Augusta being at the fortress at the time the inscription was written. Frere believed that it was Dio's hostility towards Caracalla led him to record the campaign ending in failure and not recording the true sequence of events.[97]

Malcolm Todd, however, considers there to be no evidence to support Frere's claim.[98] After Caracalla withdrew, the Caledonians retook their territory, and all remaining Romans were forced back behind Hadrian's Wall. Later expeditions beyond the wall were generally only to gather intelligence (scouting expeditions) in the area between the walls, trading contacts, bribes to purchase truces from the natives and, most importantly, the spread of Christianity. The *Ravenna Cosmography*[99] complied around 700 uses a 3rd- or 4th-century Roman map based on information gained from such scouting forays and names four markets in southern Scotland. Locus Maponi is more than likely modern Lochmabenstane, near Gretna, which was used as a muster point well into the medieval period. Two of the others name similar places used by the Damnonii and Selgovae, and the fourth, Manavi, may be Clackmannan. From the time of Caracalla onwards, however, no further attempts were made to permanently occupy territory in Scotland.

It was around the time of the withdrawal beyond Hadrian's Wall that the first recorded quote from a native of Scotland can be dated. Julia Domna, wife of Emperor Septimius Severus, apparently criticised the sexual morality of Caledonian women to which the wife of the Caledonian chief Argentocoxos allegedly is said to have replied: "We fulfil the demands of nature in a much better way than do you Roman women; for we consort openly with the best men, whereas you let yourselves be debauched in secret by the vilest".[100]

Severus's expeditions were costly in terms of casualties, which then led to Caledonian retaliations and, in the end, achieved nothing in terms of subjugating southern Scotland. However, it undoubtedly weakened the Caledonian confederacy and may, indeed, have paved the way for Irish migrants to establish themselves later in the region. For the next hundred years, the Romans concentrated instead on consolidating their position in what became the two provinces of Britannia Superior and Britannia Inferior. From the Caledonian point of view, the death of Severus initially proved timely, as it is likely that with his commitment to the conquest of Scotland, and the resources he poured into his campaigns, he would have succeeded in sweeping all opposition aside if he had lived.

As it was, the Caledonians were so weakened that they could not contemplate embarking on an immediate retaliatory campaign. The next time the term 'Caledonian' is heard of is from an

---

[96] P. 296, 'Review: "W. Gardner and H. N. Savory, *Dinorben: A Hill-Fort Occupied in Early Iron Age and Roman Times*. Cardiff: The National Museum of Wales, 196" by S. Frere (1965). *Journal of Roman Studies,* 55(November).

[97] P. 176, *Britannia: A History of Roman Britain* by S.S. Frere (1987). Routledge: London

[98] *The Northern Barbarians: 100 BC – AD 300* by M. Todd (1975) (Rev. ed. Oxford 1987).

[99] This is a list of world place names. The author is an unknown cleric form Ravenna, hence the name the *Ravenna Cosmography.*

[100] Cassius Dio, *Roman History*, LXXVII, 16.5.

inscription dated 230 from Colchester, which reads "Uepogenus, a Caledonian". Apart from this single example there are no other references to the Caledonians during the period. By the time Scotland comes back to Roman attention, the tribesmen are now referred to as Picts, with the first known use of the term occurring in 297 Despite the name-change, the Picts quickly adopted the mantle of the Caledonians and by the beginning of the 4th century were becoming a serious threat to the prosperity of northern Britain due to their unremitting raids.

The next major Roman figure to impact on the history of Scotland was the Emperor Marcus Flavius Valerius Constantius (b. c.250 – d. 306 A.D). He ruled as Caesar from 293 to 305, and as Augustus from 305 to his death, in 306. With the later empire having been divided under the Tetrarchy, introduced in 293 by Diocletian, Constantius came to rule in the west while Galerius was Augustus in the east. After his death, Constantius was given the nickname Chlorus, but is even more famous for being the father of Constantine the Great and, thus, the founder of the Constantinian dynasty. As Caesar, he defeated Carausius in Gaul and his successor, Allectus, in Britain. He also was successful fighting along the Rhine frontier, defeating both the Alamanni and Franks.

When he became Augustus, he and his son embarked on yet another punitive campaign into Scotland, this time against the Picts, who were mounting ever more destructive raids into northern England. Now the tribesmen were better organised than previously, but nonetheless, the initial Roman advance was successful. All seemed to be in place for a follow-up campaign to finally secure the region, but once again, fate intervened on the Picts' behalf. Constantius was taken ill and died unexpectedly at Eboracum in 306 Constantius's death and the acclamation of his son as Augustus by his army in the same year led to civil war and ended in the collapse of the tetrarchic system of government and the eventual overall victory of Constantine.

The situation in the empire was critical, and unsurprisingly relatively little attention was paid to the situation in northern Britain. Sporadic attempts were made to push the Picts further back from Hadrian's Wall, and efforts were made to keep it in as good repair as possible. In 343, Constans, the brother of Constantine, led an expedition that was successful for a short period in halting the attacks. However, he returned to Italy and in the following years the pattern of raids recommenced. By the mid-4th century Rome was beset by enemies on all sides. As the empire weakened, the Picts became more aggressive, and in 360, together with Irish tribesmen (the 'Scots'), they launched a major coordinated invasion of northern England. The Emperor Julian (r. 361 A.D – 363) responded by sending an army to push them back across the wall and, once again, the Picts were forced to retreat. The period of tranquillity was short lived though, and by 368 the Picts were involved in what seems to have been a highly co-ordinated series of invasions and insurrections throughout Britain.

The Roman provinces were overrun, and even London was threatened. It took fully two years for the new Emperor Valentinian (r. 364 – 375) to restore order in the south and west and to force the invading Picts and Scots back across the wall. This co-ordinated attack is known as the Great Conspiracy or the Barbarian Conspiracy. Ammianus Marcellinus, an officer in the Roman army writing twenty years after the events, is the main source for the insurrection, which he described as a "barbarica conspiratio": "The Emperor Valentinian was alarmed by serious news that Britain was brought into a state of extreme need by a conspiracy of the savages while travelling from Amiens to Treves. Count Nectaridus, general of the coastal region, had been killed; another general, Duke Fullofaudes, had been ambushed by the enemy and taken prisoner. The report alarmed the Emperor, and he sent Severus, commander of the imperial household troops, to set things right. But Severus was recalled. Another commander, Jovinus, was dispatched and he reported that a strong army was required to remedy the situation. Finally, Count Theodosius, a man with a notable war-record, was chosen to lead an expedition to Britain. He commanded four units, the Batavi, the Heruli, the Jovii, and the Victores". [101]

What is of significance about this series of attacks is the level of co-ordination and the number and range of tribes that committed themselves to fighting: "The conspiracy consisted of many barbarian tribes. The Picts, as well as the Attacotti and the Scots, were ranging widely and causing great devastation in Britain. In the Gallic regions, the Franks and their neighbours, the Saxons, harassed with cruel robbery, fire, and murder. Theodosius crossed the strait and landed at Rutupiae and began his march to Londinium".[102]

The Great Conspiracy is only mentioned by Ammianus, and given that he was writing his book during the reign of Emperor Theodosius (and that he was writing about the emperor's father!), it has to be borne in mind that his account may have been more about flattering the emperor than actual historical fact. On the other side of the coin, however, it would have been a remarkable coincidence if all the various tribes who revolted, or were involved in the invasions from the north, had acted independently and all just decided at exactly the same time to mount major offensives.

Christianity

Almost in parallel with the relative peace that Valentinian managed to achieve for a short period, the activities of one man in the south of Scotland were to prove even more significant in the evolution of Scottish history. Despite Moffat's claim that the Romans had no significant influence on the history of Scotland, even he would be hard pressed to deny that the use of the Latin script for its languages and the emergence of Christianity as the predominant religion were both major factors in shaping much of the region's cultural history. It is disingenuous to say that Christianity in Scotland owes more to Irish Celtic missionaries than it does to Roman influence, since all Christianity's success was to some extent a direct result of it becoming the imperial religion. The first major Christian figure associated with Scotland is Saint Ninian, and he was

[101] Ammianus Marcellinus, The History of the Roman Empire by Ammianus Marcellinus: During the Reigns of the Emperors Constantius, Julian, Jovianus, Valentinian, and Valens, XXVII, 8.1-10.
[102] Ibid, XXVII, 8.6,7.

not, as far as is known, Irish at all.

Tradition states that Ninian was the first bishop in Scotland. The historian Bede[103] states that the saint set up his base in 397 at Whithorn in the south-west of Scotland.[104] The church he built there, Scotland's first Christian building, was known as Candida Casa (the White Church), and around it he established a small community. This site grew in the following centuries and eventually incorporated a cathedral, a monastery, and became a major centre of pilgrimage. The centre, however, was most important as a training institution, and the monks from the White Church were a major factor in the missionary work in Scotland that eventually saw the whole region converted to Christianity.

It is known that monks from Whithorn travelled as far north as the Orkneys and Shetlands, and many of the Irish saints credited with the conversion of Ireland trained there as well. One such figure was Saint Éogan, founder of the monastery of Ardstraw, better known as the seminary of Rosnat. As well as being religious centres, these monasteries became commercial centres too, and monks from France, for example, who travelled to study at, or live in, them often brought new technology and crafts with them. This had a subtle but nonetheless important impact on local culture.

St Ninian (also known as Nynia, Ninias, Rigna, Trignan, Ninnidh, Ringan, Ninus, or Dinan) died some twenty years after the Romans left Britain, in 432 It is thought that his main successes were with the Celtic tribes but he is also credited with beginning the process of converting the Picts, a task later completed by Saint Columba and Saint Kentigern, Irish monks trained in the Whithorn tradition. There is very little in the way of hard evidence about the saint, and almost all that is known of him comes from a 12th-century life by St Aelred of Rievaulx who claimed that he was the son of a Christian Briton chieftain. He journeyed to Rome, where he was made a bishop and on his return met St Martin of Tours. However, Bede is definite that it was Ninian who initiated the conversion of the Picts.[105] He was also the first bishop of Galloway.

The fact that he was based at Whithorn is not in dispute, nor is the fact that he carried out extensive missionary work in Scotland. What is debated is the extent of his success in converting the Picts and where exactly he focused his attention. A growing consensus suggests that it was among the Celts that he found his greatest success, but what is clear from the many churches in Scotland dedicated to him is that his influence was significant there, too. The historical figure Ninian has also not yet been confirmed by irrefutable evidence, but it seems inconceivable that Bede would have invented him without some kind of historical basis. There is, however, evidence of the connection between Ireland's early saints and Whithorn. This has led historians to try to establish Bede's basis for his summary of Ninian's life.

---

[103] Also known as Saint Bede, the Venerable Bede, and Bede the Venerable.
[104] Bede, Ecclesiastical History of the English People, III, 4.
[105] Ibid.

J. H. Todd, in his publication *The Book of Hymns of the Ancient Church of Ireland* (1855), suggested that Ninian and Finnian of Moville were one and the same, and that conclusion has found favour among other academics. Finnian lived approximately 150 years after the assumed mission of Ninian, and so it is plausible that the two had been somehow mixed up in Bede's mind. Other sources that mention Ninian include the 9th-century poem *Miracula Nyniae Episcopi* that records some of the miracles attributed to him, A *Life of Saint Ninian* written around 1160 by Aelred of Rievaulx, and in 1639 James Ussher in his *Brittanicarum Ecclesiarum Antiquitates* provides quite detailed information about his life too. Aelred claimed that he had not relied totally on Bede for his information about Ninian, saying that he had a source written in a "barbarous language". Unfortunately, he did not name that source. Aelred wrote his hagiography after spending ten years at the Scottish court, and the motivation for his promotion of a specifically Scottish saint has been called into question. Indeed, T. Heffernan refers to it as a sacred biography intended for a political audience.[106]

J. Ussher, writing in the 17th century, was Archbishop of Armagh and the Primate of All Ireland. Ussher elaborated on the information provided by Bede and Aelred, claiming that Ninian moved from Candida Casa to Cluayn-coner in Ireland and died there. He also said that Ninian's mother was a Spanish princess, that he built a church using beams delivered by stags, and recounts other miracles associated with the saint. While Ussher's account is often ridiculed on the basis that he made up stories, it should be noted that he did have access to legitimate manuscripts and confirmed, or at least repeated, a number of the traditional versions of the saint's antecedents.[107]

Whether Ninian as described by Bede and others[108] existed, what is certain is that the southern area of Scotland was introduced to Christianity in the years immediately preceding the Roman withdrawal from Britain. It was those Romanized or actual Roman Christians who were in the vanguard of this missionary work, and it was their work that, in a sense, paved the way for the later Irish missionaries to complete the process. That aspect is proven by later accounts of the missions of Irish saints that can be verified. The southern Picts who Ninian is credited with converting were a mixture of Picts and the remnants of the Celtic Caledonians. Their conversion is recorded in a 5th-century Letter to Coroticus by Saint Patrick, where he calls them 'apostate Picts'. The northern Picts were not converted, however, until Saint Columba[109] arrived in the 6th century, and in using that term he acknowledges that these people had at one time been Christian.

It is clear, then, that Christianity was well established in Galloway in the 6th century, and by

---

[106] *Sacred Biography: Saints and their Biographers in the Middle Ages* by T. Heffernan (1992). Oxford. Oxford University Press.

[107] *'Britannicarum Ecclesiarum Antiquitates' by J. Ussher (1639). In: The Whole Works of the Most Reverend James Ussher, VI. Dublin.*

[108] Other authors who wrote about Saint Ninian include John Capgrave (1393–1464), John of Tinmouth (c. 1366), and John Colgan (d. c. 1657).

[109] In Ireland, he is more commonly known as Saint Colmcille.

the time Bede was writing in 731 the Northumbrians had developed a relationship with the area that had lasted more than a century. Northumbria established bishoprics subordinate to the Archbishop of York, one of which was at Whithorn in 731 The Northumbrian name given to it was *hwit œrn*, Old English for *candida casa*, all of which suggests an early and on-going Christianisation of southern Scotland. Saint Ninian's influence remained strong throughout the medieval period, and King James IV of Scotland was a regular visitor to his shrine. Saint Ninian, however, should not be given all the credit for the conversion of southern Scotland to Christianity. The finds of *chi* and *rho* tablets and Christian burial sites north of Hadrian's Wall dating from the 4th century suggest that the soldiers and ordinary Christians who lived in the vicinity of Hadrian's Wall were already active in spreading their beliefs.

Christianity had a profound impact on all parts of the empire, and to a lesser extent, the same claim can be made for those areas adjacent to the boundaries of the empire. Ninian's particular brand of Christianity based on monasticism shaped the teachings of his followers and so the specific style of Christianity adopted in Scotland. The process was circuitous, starting at Whithorn, spreading to Ireland, and then back again to Scotland from Ireland when Christianity had all but been eliminated after the withdrawal of the Romans. Christianity brought more than a religion to Scotland; it brought literacy and a commitment to education in the country that has been maintained to this day. Oxford and Cambridge were the first two universities in Britain, but they were followed by universities in Saint Andrews, Glasgow, Edinburgh and Aberdeen, all founded in the Middle Ages (while no other new university was founded in England again until Manchester in 1824).

Scotland's long tradition of education had its roots in the monastic institutions founded by Saint Ninian and his followers. By the Middle Ages, church choir schools and grammar schools had begun educating boys, and by the end of the 15th century schools were also being organised for girls. Education was encouraged by the Education Act of 1496, which made it compulsory for the sons of barons and freeholders to attend grammar schools, turning the Scottish aristocracy and middle classes into the most literate in Europe.

The Scottish Reformation (begun in 1560) saw a number of changes, including the expansion of parish school, and in the 17th century legislation set up schools in every parish. Scotland's education system made the country one of the major contributors to the Enlightenment in the 18th century, producing figures such as David Hume and Adam Smith. That culture of learning stemmed directly from the Christianisation of Scotland and the adoption of Latin as the main language of the educated, and their impact cannot be minimised. As a bona fide historical personage or not cannot diminish the significance of Ninian's image in shaping Christianity in Scotland.

Conclusion

Alistair Moffat not only dismissed the significance of the Romans in Scottish history, he also assessed their dealings with the area in the most brutal terms: "The reality is that the Romans came to what is now Scotland, they saw, they burned, killed, stole and occasionally conquered, and then they left a tremendous mess behind them, clearing away native settlements and covering good farmland with the remains of ditches, banks, roads, and other sorts of ancient military debris. Like most imperialists, they arrived to make money, to gain political advantage and to exploit the resources of their colonies at virtually any price to the conquered. And remarkably, in Britain, in Scotland, we continue to admire them for it".[110]

He is not alone in underplaying the significance of Rome on Scotland. William Hanson also asserted, "For many years it has been almost axiomatic in studies of the period that the Roman conquest must have had some major medium or long-term impact on Scotland. On present evidence that cannot be substantiated either in terms of environment, economy or, indeed, society. The impact appears to have been very limited. The general picture remains one of broad continuity, not of disruption.... The Roman presence in Scotland was little more than a series of brief interludes within a longer continuum of indigenous development".[111]

These statements may very well contain elements of truth, and if the authors had confined themselves to the statement that the Romans were unsuccessful in their attempts to conquer and Romanise Scotland, they could not be faulted. However, there is an obvious difference between that failure and the conclusion that the Romans had no significant influence on the course of Scottish history.

It is indisputable that contact with the Romans influenced every part of Scotland, up to their departure in 410, and the effects of both their prolonged period in Britain and the aftermath of their withdrawal were major factors that shaped Scotland's future, especially in its relationship with the rest of Britain. The Britons, for example, after the withdrawal, began to pay Angles and Saxons to come to their aid in repelling the increasing incursions of the Picts into northern Britain.

Indeed, it has been pointed out that, to that extent, the natives of Scotland were in large part responsible for establishing the group that was to become their greatest enemy, the English. Rome's part in that process can be seen to be an indirect one, as it was their withdrawal that created the situation, but they were still a major factor. More direct was their influence in inadvertently enabling the Picts to take control of most of Scotland by weakening many of the other tribes. The Scoti had arrived on the west coast in the years following Rome's decimation of the Caledonians, and gradually they were the ones who came to dominate the area, merging later with the Picts to create a new Scottish people.

---

[110] P. 226, *Before Scotland: The Story of Scotland Before History* by A. Moffat (2005). London. Thames & Hudson.
[111] Pp. 216, 'The Roman Presence: Brief Interludes' by W.S. Hanson (2003) In: K.J. Edwards & I.B.M. Ralston (eds). *Scotland After the Ice Age: Environment, Archaeology and History, 8000 BC – AD 1000*. Edinburgh. Edinburgh University Press.

Significant as these developments were, it can also be argued that the most important legacies of Rome were Christianity and literacy, both of which shaped a unique Scottish identity and culture. While the most enduring physical legacy left by Rome was Hadrian's Wall, which still runs more or less along the border between Scotland and England today, and which from when it was built until the present day has created a distinction between the northern part of Britain and the southern part. That physical division has contributed to a more psychological division that still has implications for politics and debates over independence and nationality – yet another more than significant Roman legacy.

Another physical legacy stems from the Romans' part in the clearances of the Caledonian forest. The 16th-century writer Hector Boece believed that the woods in Roman times stretched north from Stirling into Atholl and Lochaber.[112] Later historians such as P. F. Tytler and W. F. Skene, as well as naturalists such as F. F. Darling, have concurred with that finding.[113] The use of dendrochronology indicates that the forest was at its maximum around 3000 B.C., and deforestation may have been underway by the time the legions arrived. Nonetheless, there is clear evidence that the Roman invasion exacerbated the negative impact on the forest. The overall effect of this deforestation on the Caledonian/Pict way of life is impossible to assess, but it is certain that it must have had a tangible degree of impact.

It is true that the archaeological legacy of Rome in Scotland is sparse, especially in the north, and is almost entirely military in nature. However, there are approximately 400 miles of roads. There is no evidence that the native population either maintained them after the Romans left or adopted Roman styles of building or settlement. This is a different pattern from that observable in other parts of the empire where Roman influence is more overt. In Scotland, the basic Celtic Iron Age way of life simply re-asserted itself, and this fact is the root of the claim that the Romans had no significant influence on Scotland. However, this is over simplistic given their impact in other ways. A wider analysis of Rome's total influence on Scotland's history has to conclude that it was, indeed, significant.

Online Resources

Other books about ancient history by Charles River Editors

Other books about ancient Rome by Charles River Editors

Further Reading

Armit, I. (2003) Towers in the North: The Brochs of Scotland, Stroud: Tempus, ISBN 0-7524-1932-3

---

[112] P. 20, *A History of the Native Woodlands of Scotland 1500–1920* by T.C. Smout, R. MacDonald & F. Watson (2007). Edinburgh University Press.
[113] Ibid, pp. 20-32.

Breeze, David J. (2006) The Antonine Wall. Edinburgh. John Donald. ISBN 0-85976-655-1

Broun, Dauvit, "The Seven Kingdoms in De situ Albanie: A Record of Pictish political geography or imaginary map of ancient Alba" in E.J. Cowan & R. Andrew McDonald (eds.), (2005) Alba: Celtic Scotland in the Medieval Era. Edinburgh. John Donald. ISBN 0-85976-608-X

Byrne, Francis John (1973) Irish Kings and High-Kings. London. Batsford. ISBN 0-7134-5882-8

Carver, Martin (2008) Portmahomack: Monastery of the Picts. Edinburgh University Press. ISBN 978-0-7486-2441-6

Duncan, A.A.M (1989) Scotland: The Making of the Kingdom. The Edinburgh History of Scotland 1. Mercat Press. Edinburgh.

Forsyth, Katherine (2000) "Evidence of a lost Pictish Source in the Historia Regum Anglorum of Symeon of Durham", with an appendix by John T. Koch. pp. 27–28 in Simon Taylor (ed.) (2000). Kings, clerics and chronicles in Scotland, 500–1297: essays in honour of Marjorie Ogilvie Anderson on the occasion of her ninetieth birthday. Dublin. Four Courts Press. ISBN 1-85182-516-9

Foster, Sally M., (2004) Picts, Gaels, and Scots: Early Historic Scotland. London. Batsford. ISBN 0-7134-8874-3

Geary, Patrick J., (1988) Before France and Germany: The creation and transformation of the Merovingian World. Oxford. Oxford University Press. ISBN 0-19-504457-6

Hanson, William S. "The Roman Presence: Brief Interludes", in Edwards, Kevin J. & Ralston, Ian B.M. (Eds) (2003) Scotland After the Ice Age: Environment, Archaeology and History, 8000 BC – AD 1000. Edinburgh. Edinburgh University Press.

Keay, J. & Keay, J. (1994) Collins Encyclopaedia of Scotland. London. HarperCollins.

Kirk, William "Prehistoric Scotland: The Regional Dimension" in Clapperton, Chalmers M. (ed.) (1983) Scotland: A New Study. Newton Abbott. David & Charles.

Koch, John T. (2006) Celtic Culture: A Historical Encyclopedia. Oxford. ABC-CLIO. ISBN 1-85109-440-7

Moffat, Alistair (2005) Before Scotland: The Story of Scotland Before History. London. Thames & Hudson. ISBN 0-500-05133-X

Robertson, Anne S. (1960) The Antonine Wall. Glasgow Archaeological Society.

Smith, Beverley Ballin and Banks, Iain (2002) In the Shadow of the Brochs. Stroud. Tempus. ISBN 0-7524-2517-X

Smout, T.C. MacDonald, R. and Watson, Fiona (2007) A History of the Native Woodlands of Scotland 1500–1920. Edinburgh University Press. ISBN 978-0-7486-3294-7

Thomson, William P. L. (2008) The New History of Orkney Edinburgh. Birlinn. ISBN 978-1-84158-696-0

Woolf, Alex (2006) "Dun Nechtain, Fortriu and the Geography of the Picts" in The Scottish Historical Review, Volume 85, Number 2. Edinburgh. Edinburgh University Press.

Free Books by Charles River Editors

We have brand new titles available for free most days of the week. To see which of our titles are currently free, click on this link.

Discounted Books by Charles River Editors

We have titles at a discount price of just 99 cents everyday. To see which of our titles are currently 99 cents, click on this link.